VAT Shackles Business

VAT Shackles Business

Alex J. Dyball

authorHOUSE®

AuthorHouse™
1663 Liberty Drive
Bloomington, IN 47403
www.authorhouse.com
Phone: 1-800-839-8640

First published by AuthorHouse   01/12/2012

ISBN: 978-1-4670-0066-6 (sc)

Printed in the United States of America

Contents

Section Break

Various Accounts

- Threshold
- Return to original profit
- Hairdresser
- Convenient Store
- Etc
- French
- Templates for obtain vat liability

Contents

Foreword

What this book is all about!

Whether you're already in business or just starting up The HMRC have set guidelines for you to follow. It is said there are two sides to every story and in the business world this is very true. There is the Governments view of how things should be done and then there is the practical view of how the system actually works!

Over successive decades the government has had policies that actively promote self employment. Most people who follow this and start their own business do so because they enjoy what they are doing either because they are good at their job or it has been their hobby. Self employment in the U.K. is however a double edged sword.

When anyone is even contemplating going into business I always tell them they are throwing away a lot of legal protection. For an employed person there is Minimum Wage, four paid Holidays a year, sick pay, pension benefits and more. None of these exist for the self employed person yet they are expected to take on a lot of legal responsibilities.

Keeping financial records is something everyone expects to have to do however there is a growing list of responsibilities that have been passed from government to the self employed person. V.A.T., P.A.Y.E., N.H.I., Employment Contracts, Business Insurance, Public Liability, Health and Safety , Fire Authority's, Planning, Banking, all these have their own guidelines, laws and most importantly penalties.

As the title of this book suggests our explanations deal mainly with Value Added Tax. Our main concern is the unfair taxing of the poor I.E. the unemployed, pensioners, low incomes. Our perspective approach is from its implementation. In fact we aim to prove that it is the main cause of inflation since its UK inception on 1st April 1973. (Maurice Lauré, Joint Director of the French Tax Authority, was first to introduce VAT on April 10, 1954. In France and he was the main instigator).

We write from the UK perspective; however the EEC informs us this VAT method is used by 131 countries worldwide. It is written:-

John 8:32. "And ye shall know the truth,
and the truth shall make you free"

Truth applies to everything.

Chapter 1

This is about Government responsibility!

Over the years since 1995 when we discovered the anomaly of the Vat being excluded from the Profit and Loss Account and also realising that the Vat fraction was in fact a Sales tax fraction. We have endeavoured to rectify the problem. In fact the problem goes back to the introduction of VAT in 1973.

We have brought this problem—The difference between a Sales Tax and a Value Added tax to the Chancellor of Exchequers both Conservative and Labour, the Institute of Chartered Accountants of England & Wales, The Treasury, Office of Fair Trading, The EEC and their Department to investigate EEC irregularities. None would answer our question—especially about the vat fraction!

But in pursuing our query we also found that the forms required to calculate the tax are incorrect as to the disclosure required in EEC 6th Directive concerning exempt items

Then we discovered the application of the threshold applied to the tax is discriminating between registered and un-registered traders. it is not in the 6th Directive. Resulting in a Poverty Trap We found that combination of the different Tax rates was also creating confusion.

Ultimately, we have concluded that especially for caterers to pay the sales tax the way imposed by HMRC they can only make a profit if they falsify their accounts or to put it in HMRC terminology BLACK ECONOMY. That is why caterers are prime targets for investigation.

1

Alex J. Dyball

The outcome of all these accumulated problems has created Hardship, Unemployment, Bankruptcies and untold misery to literally millions of people. Also, according to our correspondence received from the EEC—They tell us it is being wrongly applied in 131 Countries.

The following Waterfall Charts indicate VAT is a significant reason that most UK companies suffer from limited expansion. Sectors such as Banking, Insurance, Passenger Transport and Utilities supply have considerable less restriction for growth based on their VAT status.

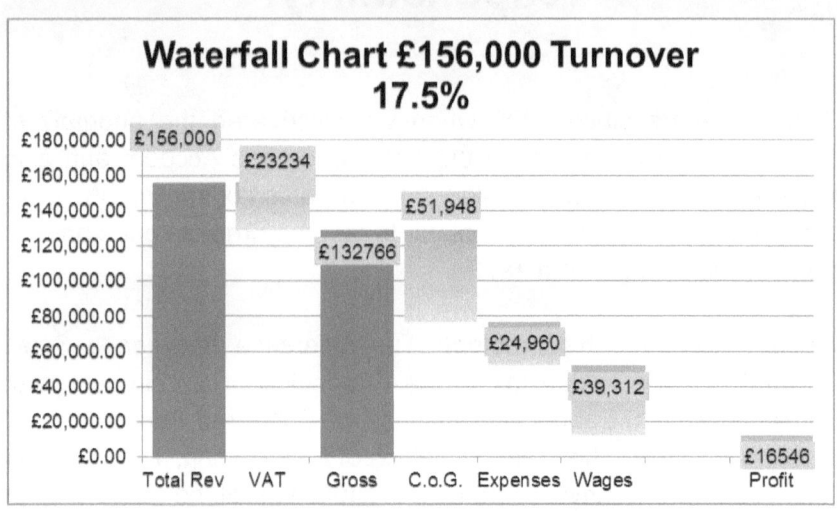

The above chart depicts any business with a gross yearly turnover of £156,000. For this business the following applies:—

HMRC states the business owes 7/47ths of £156,000 = £23234 Vat

Or simply put

Vat +Income Tax	17% = £ 26,543	(£23,234+£3309 income Tax)[*1]
Wages..............	25% = £ 39,312	
Overheads	16% = £ 24,960	
Cost of Goods	33.5% = £ 51,948	
	£ 142,763	
Net Profit after Tax	8.5% £ 13,237	
	100% £ 156,000.	**WHO SUFFERS?**

2

At present Vat has increased to 20% however turnover remained the same at £156,000 as can be seen on the chart below. But history has shown that increasing prices reduces demand—or to be fair people only have the same amount of money in their pockets so they cannot buy.

Vat is now 1/6th of £156,000 = £26.000—

Vat +Income Tax	18% = £ 28,650	(£26,000+£2650 income Tax)[2]
Wages…………..	25% = £ 39,312	
Overheads	16.5%	£ 25,490
Cost of Goods	33.5%	£ 51,948
		£ 145,400
Net Profit after Tax	7%	£ 10,600
	100%	£156,000. **WHO SUFFERS?**

Wages have stayed the same but expenses have increased due to vat new level to £25,490. Cost of goods (net tax) stay the same (?) £51,948. Shareholders portion now £13250 less income tax £2650 = £10,600. So Govt. gets £28650(18%) Staff (25%) Expenses (16.5%) C .o. G (33.5%), shareholders (7%), £212 per week (for their capital Investment) whilst HMRC get £573.(No investment and obligations whatsoever) Sure the Gov't want you self-employed and you take all the risk, investment and make you do their work keeping the records to pay them—**WHY ARE BUSINESSES CLOSING?** They are top heavy keeping records filing in forms etc. The United Kingdom was known as a nation of shopkeepers—now it is book-keepers.

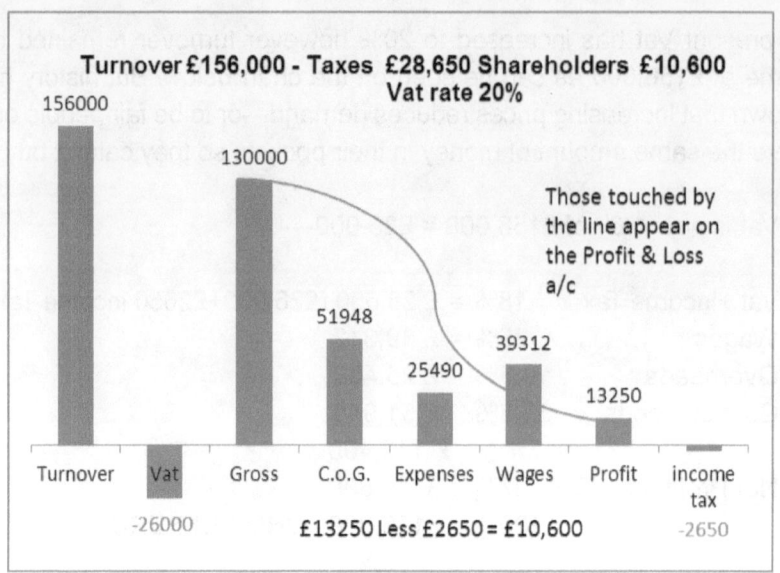

Turnover £156,000 - Taxes £28,650 Shareholders £10,600
Vat rate 20%

Those touched by the line appear on the Profit & Loss a/c

So in a nutshell the Government have increased the VAT from 17.5% to 20% an increase of 14.28%. In the above example we watched the shareholders earnings go down from £13,237 to £10,600 a reduction of 19.9%. Is it any wonder the country is in such a mess? Can you tell us how business is to absorb a 34% swing? In spite of what anyone tells you it is not a consumer tax. It is financial suicide!

[1]   When VAT is 17.5% Goods £132,766 (100%) Vat £23,234 (17.5%) = £156,000 (117.5%)
[2]   When Vat is 20% Goods £130,000 (100%) Vat £26,000(20%) = £156,000(120%)

Now every business must pay vat. We start by giving a simple example here. Heating Oil or Gas Cylinder.

Sells to the consumer for £30-00(100%) + VAT £1-50(5%) =Total £31-50. Buys from supplier for £20-00(100%) + VAT £4-00(20%) =Total £24-00. So this means the independent supplier of the Oil or Gas collects a refund of £2-50 net from the HMRC. How is this reflected in their Profit & Loss Account? How is this tax on their value added? He has added £10.a 5% tax on that is 50p—so he virtually is better off by £3-00!

Chapter 2

The truth about Value added tax.

Truth.

Let us first accept a biblical fact "All knowledge is not truth
but all truth is knowledge!"

As we explained in the foreword – VAT was first implemented by a
Frenchman in France in 1954. Although it was the German industrialist
Dr. Wilhelm von Siemens who invented the concept in 1918, It was
also used by Lord Weinstock of the English General Electric Company
in establishing GEC costing's he used Added Value. We mention this
to assure people that it is not a concept originating with the EEC as
such.

Now at the outset let us remember there is only one "Value Added Tax
Act 1994" this is to convey the content of the "6th Directive of EEC". This
one Act is to cover all businesses and their activities *not the consumer*.
The 6th Directive is implemented in every EEC country but is translated
into each country's own Legislation.

When we say businesses it is meant to cover all commercial transactions
– Banks, Insurance, Retailers, Transport, Supermarkets, Golf Clubs,
Restaurants, Solicitors, Plumbers, Builders, etc . . . . However, every
business has differing requirements. E.g. a solicitor will need a computer
as a main piece of equipment but a Plumber would have more use for
a pipe bender. Banks goods are money, whereas a Restaurant is food.
Each business is like a garden – it needs, tools, seeds, etc. all are
different. For a vegetable garden you would need a cultivator, whereas

with a lawn, a mower and this mower are dependent on the size of the Garden.

So we have set the scene now for your business! You're just starting up as a lawyer; you need an office, computer, Stationery and a law degree. Starting up as a Plumber, you need a Van, Blow torch, copper pipes, served as apprentice etc. You do not need an office – you work from home.

Now without a business then value added tax will _not exist_. In fact without business jobs would _not exist_. In fact Government would _not exist_. (Although with politicians you would get the impression without them nothing could be done! They create employment or is it bureaucracy?) So the next question is what is value added. So we turn to the source of our knowledge. In Europe being English we turn to someone in the UK. Well then we have the expertise to consider – so our selection of candidate is Professor John Kay of the London School of Economics. He has written a book called "Foundations of Corporate Success" In this book he states that Value Added is "Outputs less Inputs on a Cash Basis (ignoring depreciation)". To be more specific it is the same for a Street stall Trader and Debenhams, this is Profits plus Wages to keep it simple on a cash basis. In the case of countries this is called GDP – they obtain this figure by adding all the wages paid out for every citizen and add the profits of corporations. With a sole trader like a Lawyer their earnings less expenses leaves profits, which is their Value Added.

Let us at the beginning dispel the myth that it is a consumer tax. It is passed on to the consumer as are all taxes – e.g. Corporation tax is levied on business profits but this is absorbed in the prices charged to consumers. But as to the responsibility to pay it always falls on the business. (Including NHI and PAYE)

From the EEC point of view the GDP of each member state is assessed at 1% and this is sent to Brussels. This same condition has also been applied to all new members

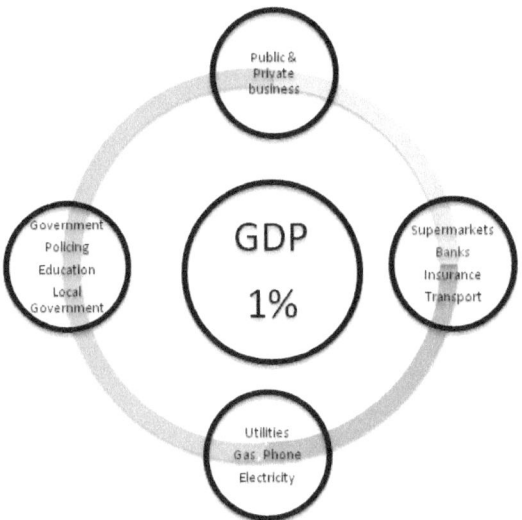

Public and
Private
Businesses

Private business such as Bin Collection can compete with Public Business supplying the same service. Exhibitions or places of interest are another section where they compete against one another. This red section is all taxed the same at standard rate which is at present in 2010 @ 17.5%. The biggest contributors to this section are Manufacturing (Cars, Furniture), Building Industry and Retail Shops.

Supermarkets,
Banks, Insurance
Transport

These four categories of business are mainly taxed as EXEMPT – This means for example that Transport which uses diesel can reclaim the standard rated tax it has paid. Insurance is liable to an Insurance Premium Tax but it is not reclaimable against vat. Supermarkets are not exempt but are classed as "zero rated" on food. Tax Inspectors cannot differentiate between "Exempt" and "zero rate" (They say it is a rate of tax which is zero – numerically speaking) BUT not explaining how they are treated on a Vat return! Notice transport includes Air Travel – so other charges like Airport tax is added – which of course cannot be reclaimed. Incidentally, under EEC law exempt amounts should be disclosed on the Vat 100 form but it is not – so Outputs include this amount so there is no way of distinguishing the basis for Value added (Taxable Outputs less taxable Inputs).

Government
Policing Education
Local Government

These categories are all exempt and have reciprocal agreements not to charge vat between departments – but if charging the public they are to add vat at standard rate – example admission to swimming pool. Another example is if a Solicitor is acting for any of these Government Departments they do not charge them vat.

Utilities
– Gas
–Electricity
–Phone

The phone utility charges vat at standard rate – but Gas & Electricity are at the reduced rate which is at present 5%.

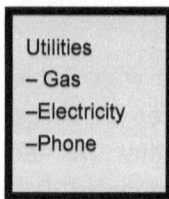

GDP
1%

This is the Big Ball of WAX – TAX!

Now regardless in which section above the wages, salaries or profits is made they are all added together and this represents the GNP or in another terminology (VALUE ADDED of the Country). The Governments collect the most of their vat income from business  and the utilities  and since it is 17.5% and 5%—you can see they are subsidising earnings of Government – Banking – Education – Transport. So it is a waxy (sticky) situation—with anomalies which distort competition. We will refer to this later to explain how it creates deceitful accountability.

It is written Ephesians 6:12. "For we wrestle not against flesh and blood, but against principalities, against powers, against the rulers of the darkness of this world, against spiritual wickedness in high places."

This scripture is quoted because the EEC Commission is not elected by the peoples – the European Parliament is elected but the Commission is not.

To obtain the basis of vat from a modern source we go to Encarta:

Definitions obtained from Encarta.

Value Added Tax, (VAT), a tax on <u>consumption</u> that is levied whenever goods and services change hands in the course of <u>production</u>, <u>distribution</u>, and final <u>sale</u> to the consumer.

For example, a manufacturer pays VAT on the materials it buys to make a product, the wholesaler pays VAT on the price it pays the manufacturer for the good, the retailer pays VAT on the price it pays the wholesaler, and the price paid by the consumer also includes VAT. Ultimately, it is the consumer who carries the burden of the tax because all those in the process up to the final sale are liable, when <u>accounting</u> to the tax authorities, to[i] deduct the VAT they have paid on their inputs from the VAT they have collected on their outputs. So, the manufacturer can deduct the VAT paid on materials from the VAT collected from the wholesaler. The idea is that at every stage <u>value</u> is added, tax is levied on the amount of value added. [ii]This distinguishes it from a sales tax, which is simply a tax on the retail price of goods.

Sales Tax, <u>taxation</u> imposed on the sale of goods or services. The tax is computed as a percentage of the total <u>sales price</u>. Sales taxes may be imposed either on the purchaser or on the seller; in the former case they are charged on each transaction and in the latter they are collected as a percentage of the gross receipts during a given period. A sales tax differs from an excise in that the sales tax is imposed on the sales transaction rather than on the article of commerce as such. Sales taxes are common throughout the world, a notable example being the value added tax levied throughout the European Union[iii]. They are not universally popular, especially when introduced on top of existing tax regimens: the introduction of a sales tax in Japan in 1988 met with widespread disapproval.

*The point we want to establish here is that Encarta quite rightly points out that the Vat levied throughout the E.U. is a Sales tax – not our opinion but Encarta's. So it clarifies our opinion that it is **NOT** a Value added tax.*

So then we come to the Law or the UK Governments power of authority:

> 1. Chapter 23 of the VATA 1994 clearly states Part I:3 (1) "A person is a taxable person for the purposes of this Act while he is, or is required to be, registered under this Act".

Now it is perfectly obvious that the government cannot take the public to court. Therefore vat as is stated in the Act is correct. The Business (he) is the responsible taxpayer. (Taxable Person) Do you agree? There is only one VATA 1994 so it covers all businesses so the liability for vat or rules governing the liability must be universal (applied equally to all).

> The VATA 1994 states Chapter 23 Part I: 1 (2) Vat on any supply of goods or services is a liability of the person making the supply and becomes due at the time of the supply. *Now this is not the responsibility or the liability of the customer/ the consumer it is the supplier. But under the provisions of the Act the business recovers the vat **charged** at each stage from the customer/and passes it on eventually to the consumer.*

This raises two points which are not authorised in the Customs & Revenue guidelines.

1. *The business can only pass on what it has been <u>charged</u>? (recovers at each stage)*

However, HMRC use *"7/47ths of the selling price"*. They call a "Vat Fraction" depicts a value distorted by Government method of application Thereby, it is illegally charging vat and also vat is being applied on exempt and lower rated items.[iv]

A "Vat fraction" a phrase or term not in the VATA 1994 or the 6th Directive.

2. "Registration of a taxable person is specified in the Act. As is shown in marked item 1 above.
3. *At present (2010) this is stated as at £70,000. However, it does not say that a business earning under that figure cannot register.*

The ambiguity arises when a business crosses over this figure called the Threshold. Since the business under £70,000 is not liable to vat unless it registers. But as its Selling prices are the same as a registered business it is recovering any vat it has paid on its purchases and the output vat is in effect being charged to the consumer and unregistered business is pocketing extra profit!

This is not just a United Kingdom problem it is EEC wide.

How do we come to this conclusion – well in the first place the EEC office has told us a vat fraction is used throughout the world in 131 countries. We asked "does that prove it (the method) to be correct?" but we did not receive a reply to that question.

Secondly, it was reported in the English press-

In December 2005, Tony Blair went to a European Union summit in Brussels and agreed to a big increase in Britain's net payments to the EU budget—from the current level of £3.5 billion a year, to over £6 billion a year.[v] **This is an astonishing £115 million every week, even taking into account the money we receive back from the EU in grants and subsidies.**

Blair agreed to this increase despite regular reports of EU fraud, despite failing to reform the EU's wasteful Common Agricultural Policy and despite the "inability of auditors to approve the EU's accounts for 12 years running." Ms Marta Andreasen, the EU's former chief accountant, was sacked by then EU Commissioner for revealing that: She stated

> *"Opportunities for fraud are open and they are taken advantage of. The most elementary precautions are neither taken nor even contemplated"*

Mathew 12:25-26 Jesus said "Every Kingdom divided against its self is brought to desolation and every city or house divided against its self will not stand. If Satan casts out Satan he is divided against himself. How then will his Kingdom stand?"

What the bible is stating here is that you cannot police yourself!

E.E.C. Influence on National Taxation.

We would at this point like to draw attention to another point concerning the 6th Directive. As we said earlier all countries pay 1% on the countries GNP. But allow all individual countries to establish their own rates provided they do not exceed 25%. As we explained it is the earnings of everyone from Royalty, MP's, Civil Servants, NH Service, Teachers, Police, Traffic Wardens, Banks, Insurance, Social Workers, Council Workers, and Supermarkets, Farmers, Fishermen. Apart from the last 3 aforementioned all their occupations are exempt and the last 3 are zero rated. Now in Northern Ireland 736,000 people are in work between the ages of 16-65. Of that number 35% are in Public Administration of Education & Health and I understand that the Government employs approximately 60% of the working Population (Police are not included below).

The next section is a computation based upon everybody working 40 hours at the minimum wage of £6. The persons working are from Governments published figures concerning Northern Ireland. Below you will see Northern Ireland's contribution to EEC is £1,748,736. Whereas, the Government collects £15,526,656 from business **Per Week**

	Northern Ireland Workforce			weekly		
	Taken off website	£240	40 hrs.		Paid out	collected
Perc%	Between ages of 16 to 65	£6	Mini Wage		EEC 1%	20%/5%
1	Energy & Water (0) (all treated as 5%)	7360	£1,766,400		£1,766	£88,320
2.8	Agriculture, forestry & fishing	20608	£4,945,920		£49,459	Zero
11.5	Manufacturing	84640	£20,313,600		£203,136	£4,062,720
9.4	Construction	69184	£16,604,160		£166,042	£3,320,832
19.5	Distribution, Hotels & Rest.	143520	£34,444,800		£344,448	£6,888,960
6.6	Transport & Communication	48576	£11,658,240		£116,582	£1,165,824
11.2	Banking & finance	82432	£19,783,680		£197,837	Exempt
34.3	Public Admin, Education	252448	£60,587,520		£605,875	Exempt
3.6	Services(supermarkets assumed)	26496	£6,359,040		£63,590	zero
99.9		735264	£176,463,360.00		**£1,748,736**	£15,526,656
	Average annual income	52	£12,480			
	Transport Exempt so we used >>	10%	Weekly Government Profit			£13,777,920.00

	Belfast	Outer Belfast	East of NI	North of NI	West & South of NI	Northern Ireland
Agriculture, forestry and fishing (%)	*	*	3.9	*	5.3	2.8
Energy and water (%)	*	*	*	*	*	1.0
Manufacturing (%)	6.3	8.6	14.2	9.7	15.4	11.5
Construction (%)	*	7.3	8.6	11.7	13.9	9.4
Distribution, hotels and restaurants (%)	20.7	18.0	21.2	22.9	16.3	19.5
Transport and communication (%)	9.9	8.2	6.1	5.9	4.3	6.6
Banking and finance (%)	15.1	16.3	10.0	8.3	7.2	11.2
Public admin, education and health (%)	37.2	36.7	31.9	34.1	33.2	34.3
Other services (%)	6.2	*	3.4	*	*	3.6
Total (000's)	99	165	199	107	167	736

Alex J. Dyball

The above chart was taken off Government website it was converted to money by assuming the minimum wage applies to everyone – and that is a weekly profit

---

(1) his expression is different to the 6th Directive & VATA 1994 where they state money charged can be **PASSED ON to the consumer**. Is this a question of phraseology?

(2) This emphasis's the difference between it and a Sales tax. The point being if it is zero or exempt or Lower rate it cannot be passed on as standard rate

(3) Although I have continually stressed to HMRC and the Treasury that they apply a **Sales tax** they deny it. But this confirms I am correct.

(4) A typical example of this is NIES charges 17.5% on its bills whilst Calor Gas charges 5%. NIES says it is because it is for Commercial businesses and a HMRC dictate. So if this applies to Electricity why does it not apply to GAS? Or is it they gain extra interest on the money until they pay the Government. Where is the legality basis for this HMRC dictate?

(5) In present day terms 2010 we are 5x£6 billion out of pocket – maybe this is a part of the reason for the Present deficit they are quoting!

Chapter 3

EEC Website.

The following was taken off the European Commission website.

The 6th Directive, Article 22
Obligations under the internal system

1. Every taxable person shall state when his activity as a taxable person commences, changes or ceases.
2. Every taxable person shall keep accounts in sufficient detail to permit application of the value added tax and inspection by the tax authority.
3. (a) Every taxable person shall issue an invoice, or other document serving as invoice in respect of all goods and services supplied by him to another taxable person, and shall keep a copy thereof.
Every taxable person shall likewise issue an invoice in respect of payments on account made to him by another taxable person before the supply of goods or services is affected or completed.
(1) (b) The invoice shall state clearly the price exclusive of tax and the corresponding tax at each rate as well as any exemptions.
(c) The Member States shall determine the criteria for considering whether a document serves as an invoice.
4. Every taxable person shall submit a return within an interval to be determined by each Member State. This interval may not exceed two months following the end of each tax period. The tax period may be fixed by Member States as a month, two months, or a quarter. However, Member States may fix different periods provided that these do not exceed a year.

The return must set out all the information needed to calculate the tax that has become chargeable and the deductions to be made, including, where appropriate, and in so far as it seems necessary for the establishment of the tax basis, the total amount of the transactions relative to such tax and deductions,[2] and the total amount of the exempted supplies.

5. Every taxable person shall pay the net amount of the value added tax when submitting the return. The Member States may, however, fix a different date for the payment of the amount or may demand an interim payment.

6. Member States may require a taxable person to submit a statement, including the information specified in paragraph 4, and concerning all transactions carried out the preceding year. This statement must provide all the information necessary for any adjustments.

7. Member States shall take the necessary measures to ensure that those persons who, in accordance with Article 21 (1) (a) and (b), are considered to be liable to pay the tax instead of a taxable person established in another country or who are jointly, and severally liable for the payment, shall comply with the above obligations relating to declaration and payment.

8. Without prejudice to the provisions to be adopted pursuant to Article 17 (4), Member States may impose other obligations which they deem necessary for the correct levying and collection of the tax and for the prevention of fraud.

9. Member States may release taxable persons:—from certain obligations,
   - From all obligations where those taxable persons carry out only exempt transactions,
   - From the payment of the tax due where the amount is insignificant.

Article 23
Obligations in respect of imports

As regards imported goods, Member States shall lay down the detailed rules for the making of the declarations and payments.

In particular, Member States may provide that the value added tax payable on importation of goods by taxable persons or persons liable to tax or certain categories of these two need not be paid at the time of importation, on condition that the tax is mentioned as such in a return to be submitted under Article 22 (4).

Also from the website.
How is it charged? (Underlined parts by Alex Dyball—proving their words)

The VAT due on any sale is a percentage of the sale price but from this the taxable person is entitled to deduct all the tax already paid at the preceding stage. Therefore, double taxation is avoided and [3] **tax is paid** only on the value added at each stage of production and distribution. In this way, as the final price of the product is equal to the sum of the values added at each preceding stage, the final VAT paid is made up of the sum of the VAT paid at each stage.

Registered VAT traders are given a number and have [4]to show the VAT charged to customers on invoices. In this way, the customer, if he is a registered trader, knows how much he can deduct in turn and the consumer knows how much tax he has paid on the final product. In this way the correct VAT is paid in stages and to a degree the system is self-policing. The system operates as follows:

Example

Stage 1

A mine sells iron ore to a smelter. The sale is worth €1000 and, if the VAT rate is 20%, the mine charges its customers €1200. It should pay €200 to the treasury, but as it has bought €240 worth of tools in the same accounting period, including €40 VAT, it is only required to pay €160 (€200 less €40) to the treasury. The treasury also receives the €40 and now gets €160 making €200—which is the correct amount of VAT due on the sale of the iron ore.

Alex J. Dyball

- Supply: €1000
- VAT on supply: €200
- VAT on purchases: €40
- Net VAT to be paid: €160

Stage 2

The smelter has paid €200 VAT to the mine and, say, another €20 VAT on other purchases, such as furniture, stationery, etc. So when the smelter sells €2000 worth of steel it charges €2400 including €400 VAT. The smelter deducts the €220 already paid on his inputs and pays €180 to the treasury. The treasury receives this €180 from the smelter plus €160 from the mine, plus €40 paid by the supplier of tools to the mine, plus €20 paid by the furniture/stationary supplier to the smelter.

- Supply: €2.000
- VAT on supply: €400
- VAT on purchases: €220
- Net VAT to be paid: €180

	This is our summary of Value added tax above.				20%		Output	How
	Inputs			Outputs		Total	Less	Paid
	Buys	Vat	Total Cost	Sells	Vat	Sell Price	Input	To HMRC
Tools Mine				200	40	240	40	40
Mine	200	40	240	1000	200	1200	160	160
Smelter Furniture -	1000	200	1200	1100	220	1320	20	20
Smelter	1100	220	1320	2000	400	2400	180	180
Consumer	2000	400	2400			Total paid		400

€180 (paid by the smelter) + €160 (paid by the mine) + €40 (paid by the supplier to the mine) + €20 (paid by the supplier to the smelter) = €400 or the correct amount of VAT on a sale worth €2000.

We have constructed this as a Tables below in keeping with our own interpretation.

18

(1) This should be reflected on the UK VAT 100 form. **Exemptions are not stated.** Restaurant's Receipt later does not state price exclusive of tax. But inclusive with tax

(2) This is the point I make in Comment 1 above. The UK Return Vat 100 form does not allow for exempt.

(3) This stresses that tax is paid at each stage—Exempt—cannot be added. Zero cannot be added & Lower rate can only be added at that rate, not as a Standard Rate.

(4) Again I refer to Restaurant's Invoice which the author received for goods purchased. It has no reflection on the Restaurant's business.

Tools Mine		
Sells @	£240	
Buys @	£0	
Value Added including tax		£240
Made up off VA	£200	
Sales tax/VAT?	£40	

Mine		
Sells @	£1200	
Buys @	£240	
Value Added including tax		£960
Made up off VA	£800	
Sales tax/VAT?	£160	

Smelter Furniture		
Sells @	£1320	
Buys @	£1200	
Value Added including tax		£120
Made up off VA	£100	
Sales tax/VAT?	£20	

Smelter		
Sells @	£2400	
Buys @	£1320	
Value Added including tax		£1080
Made up off VA	£900	
Sales tax/VAT?	£180	

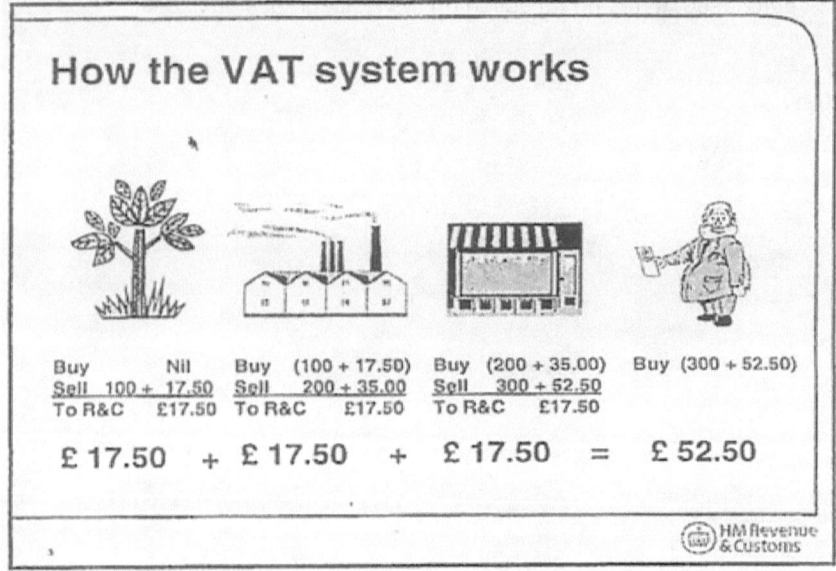

How the VAT system works

Buy   Nil   Buy (100 + 17.50)   Buy (200 + 35.00)   Buy (300 + 52.50)
Sell 100 + 17.50   Sell 200 + 35.00   Sell 300 + 52.50
To R&C £17.50   To R&C £17.50   To R&C £17.50

£17.50 + £17.50 + £17.50 = £52.50

HM Revenue & Customs

This is HMRC leaflet conveying the 6th Directive outlined above although they are using a different business.(R&C is Revenue and Customs)

Now with no disrespect to our Universities but the going pass rate in Mathematics' is 30%. If it is that percentage for them the average layman would naturally be lower so when it comes to figures(mathematics) you'll know the average person is not good.(see confirming article below)

General observations.

On 6th April'05 at the Public Accounts Committee of the House of Commons it was observed that 26 Million Adults have a numeric & literacy deficiency. When you consider the population of the UK is 59.6 Million and approximately 16 Million of them are under 20. This leaves 43.6 Million and if 26 Million of them have numeric problems this represents 60% of all adults and nearly 44% of total population. It is also a know fact that 70% of university students are deficient in math. So assuming this is the 20 year Olds (16Million x 70%) 11.2Million. Total persons with numeric deficiency are 37.2 million that's 62.4% of the general public. Namely two out of three, so is it any wonder that people do not understand VAT. How many MP's are there in Parliament? How many of them understand figures let alone vat?

Then we come to the Blue Paper for the year 2003, £77864 Million is paid in Vat and we are 52 Billion in debt. But my point here is it clearly states "GDP measures the sum of the value added created through the production of goods and services within the economy"

Talking Fractions or Percentages!

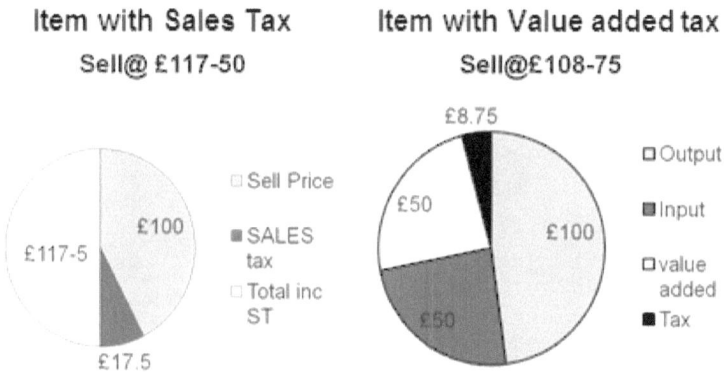

Who gets the other £8-75 and who is out of pocket?

There is a precedent set by the EEC concerning individual Governments not conforming to EEC legislation. A directive is described in article 189 of the treaty of Rome as "binding as to the results to be achieved, upon each member state to which it is addressed, but shall leave to the national authorities the choice of form and methods. *But we point out here that the above method and calculations for VAT came from the EEC 6th Directive and is their website example.* The European

Alex J. Dyball

Court of Justice has also held in a number of cases that directives can be relied upon directly in the courts.

The clearest expression of this was the precedent case in Holland in1977, brought by the Federation of Dutch Industries, and relating to a minor detail of the 2nd VAT Directive. The Dutch VAT laws had a slightly different meaning. The European Court held that, although the Community rule was only a directive, the taxpayer could rely on it, rather than the national law which brought the Community Law into effect in Holland. There are Community directives on banking, insurance, doctors and nurses, lawyers, companies, rights of workers, adulteration of food, consumer protection etc. So what we are saying is the above directive can be relied on. Therefore our figures are right and can be relied upon as representing what the EEC website has decreed as an example.

```
            VAT number 036 2012 792
        Your operator today isANNE
          14/07/2006 at 01:50 pm
        Transaction Number 275092 on Till 1
-------------------------------------------------
Pump 10: Diesel
   20.64 L. @ 96.9 p =          £20.00

                    TOTAL = £20.00

                CASH PAID = £20.00
-------------------------------------------------
VAT Rate NET Price  V.A.T. Gross Price
 17.5%    17.02      2.98     20.00
-------------------------------------------------
        Thank you for your custom
            Please Call Again
```

(v)   This copy of a fuel docket states the price paid as £20 (including vat) but is in fact a Sales tax. Since £2-98 is 17.5% on the selling price of £17.02. In fact the amount stated is petrol supplier's vat plus whatever it has paid to its supplier. The next "General observations" shown above is the basis not of our observation but the Governments on numeracy ability.

Below are random invoices made by suppliers—followed by the P100 form which does not conform to the 6th Directive concerning exempt items!

```
            TAX INVOICE


#01 Order No.: 0370 #POS/EJ Order: 2602
    REG  3    18/09/2008 19:42:36

QTY ITEM                        TOTAL

 1 2 cheese & 2 med fr          2.50
 1 M-STRAW SHK                  1.29
 1 DOUBLE CHB                   1.49

Total                          5.28
Cash                          10.00
Change                         4.72

         TAX %         AMOUNT
VAT      17.500         5.28
NOVAT     0.000         0.00
    TOTAL AMOUNT        5.28

    Phone:        02890-866551
    VAT Number:   802793822
```

```
                TAX INVOICE


#01 Order No.: 0040 #POS/EJ Order: 6468
    REG  4-   09/10/2008 11:01:06

QTY ITEM                        TOTAL

 1 DOUBLE CHB                    1.19
>>01 WELDON

Total                           1.19
Cash                            1.20
Cashback                        0.01

          TAX %          AMOUNT
VAT       17.500          1.19
NOVAT      0.000          0.00
     TOTAL AMOUNT         1.19

     Phone: 02825 632330
       VAT: 371057172
```

```
        PALMA DE MALLORCA
        C.I.F A-4001649-E

            TICKET

#ORD 0022 -CAJ 7- 16/08/2008 09:44:06
UND ARTC
   1 SPRITE P                   TOTAL
                                 1.50
Total Tomar (incl IVA)          1.50
EUR                             1.50

TOTAL INCLUIDO IVA DE           7.00%
0.10
```

The top two receipts are in Northern Ireland and have individual tax numbers & the third is in Mallorca—Spain. As you can see the Vat amount is not stated except in Mallorca—7% would in our estimation be the correct Value added tax. (Now 8%) although it is also a Sales tax and is lower because it is classed as a lower rate food item in Spain.

Spain increases VAT rate from 16% to 18%

March 14 2010 As part of a range of deficit cutting austerity measures, Spain will increase its VAT rate from 16% to 18% from 1 July 2010.

Standard Rate 18% (since 1 July 2010)
Reduced Rate 8%

---

(1) This gives an example of a Cash Receipt—separating Tax & goods. However, we would point out it is a **SALES TAX** since it is based upon the selling price.

Alex J. Dyball

This is the form which does not show **"EXEMPT"** Items on it as directed by the EEC. So how can the firms liability be confirmed simply?

		£	p
For official use	VAT due in this period on sales and other outputs	**1**	
	VAT due in this period on acquisitions from other EC Member States	**2**	
	Total VAT due (the sum of boxes 1 and 2)	**3**	
	VAT reclaimed in this period on purchases and other inputs (including acquisitions from the EC)	**4**	
	Net VAT to be paid to Customs or reclaimed by you (Difference between boxes 3 and 4)	**5**	
	Total value of sales and all other outputs excluding any VAT. Include your box 8 figure	**6**	00
	Total value of purchases and all other inputs excluding any VAT. Include your box 9 figure	**7**	00
	Total value of all supplies of goods and related costs, excluding any VAT, to other EC Member States	**8**	00
	Total value of all acquisitions of goods and related costs, excluding any VAT, from other EC Member States	**9**	00

Value Added Tax Return

For the period
01 05 07 to 31 07 07

HM Customs and Excise

For Official Use

Registration Number   Period
                                  07 07

You could be liable to a financial penalty if your completed return and all the VAT payable are not received by the due date.

Due date: 31 08 07

For Official Use

If you have a general enquiry or need advice please call our National Advice Service on 0845 010 9000

Before you fill in this form please read the notes on the back and the VAT leaflets *"Filling in your VAT return"* and *"Flat rate scheme for small businesses"*, if you use that scheme. Fill in all boxes clearly in ink, and write 'none' where necessary. Don't put a dash or leave any box blank. If there are no pence write "00" in the pence column. Do not enter more than one amount in any box.

DECLARATION: You, or someone on your behalf, must sign below.

If you are enclosing a payment please tick this box.

I, ... declare that the
            (Full name of signatory in BLOCK LETTERS)
information given above is true and complete.

Signature .... Date ....
            A false declaration can result in prosecution

B

0003348
VAT 100 (full)   Page 1   PT1 (September 2004) (02/07)

24

Chapter 4

What this book will mean to you.

1. If you are a Value Added Tax registered Business.
2. If you are a Caterer.

The value added tax laws are very complicated this is a deliberate ploy used by Government so the average man in the street cannot question it, similar to the Family Tax Credits and other legislation. In fact we may have gone over earlier ground again. If so excuse us since we want to cover everything. It is written Hosea 4:6 "My people are destroyed for lack of knowledge"

To cut through all the legislation we have placed it in our book for reference so you can establish where we get the authority for our argument.

Threshold
All registered businesses.

This is referred to in VATA 1994 23rd Chapter Part 1.3 (1) "A person is a taxable person for the purposes of this Act while he is, or is required to be, registered under this Act".

(a) Registration of a taxable person is specified in the Act. As is shown in marked item 1 above. *At present (2010) this is stated as at £70,000. However, it does not say that a business earning under that figure cannot register.*

The ambiguity arises when a business crosses over this figure called the **Threshold.** So at this point we want to emphasis that a threshold is an entrance point—e.g. carry your wife over the threshold. However, in tax terms there are 3 precedents (a law established by following earlier judicial decisions) set by Government when people enter into tax as a taxpayer. (Part 1.3 above highlighted states that a person is a TAXABLE PERSON).

1. In income tax the first <u>threshold</u> is £6475 for personal allowance and every adult is entitled to earn below this before paying tax. When you earn £6500 less personal allowance you are liable to £25 X 10% = £2-50 income tax. **Not £650.00**

2. In N.H.I. there is a <u>threshold</u> of £97 and the rate of NHI is 11%. So if you earn £120 less lower rate £97 you are liable to £23 x 11% = £2.53. **Not £13.20**

3. Inheritance tax <u>Threshold</u> Nil tax band £325,000 and the tax is 40% over that amount. So again if your estate is £425,000 your liability is £100,000 X 40% = £40,000. **Not £170,000**

4. So now we come to the bit that applies to all registered for Vat businesses. HMRC says you do not have to register for vat until you reach £70,000. (So by stating this condition in that phraseology it establishes the Act covers all businesses. We know of a business that is under £70,000 that is registered). Then you have to apply the "vat fraction"—now this term is not in the VATA 1994 but it is HMRC interpretation of how vat is calculated. It appears in their Notice 727 page 50. Reproduced below:—

Appendix A   The VAT fraction

---

1. Why do I need to know about the VAT fraction ?	Because the price you charge your customer usually includes VAT, you will have to work out how much of it is actually VAT. To do this, you need the VAT fraction.

For example, if you sell something at £2.35 and the VAT rate is 17.5%, the amount of VAT is 35p. But 35 is not 17.5% of £2.35, it is 7/47 of £2.35. This is how it is worked out:

$$\frac{\text{rate of tax}}{100 + \text{rate of tax}}$$

So with VAT at 17.5% the VAT fraction is:

$$\frac{17.5}{117.5} = 7/47$$

2. What if the rate of tax changes ?	If the rate of tax changes there will be a new VAT fraction which you will have to use in your scheme calculations. This will be publicised at the time c a rate change, but you can work it out for yourself by using the method set out above.

First we point out that the fraction above is a **SALES TAX FRACTION.** Selling something at £2-00 which is the Sales price and a 17.5% Sales tax would be 35p.

This statement is correct! Prove us wrong.

To obtain a value added tax you would have to know the Input Value. So if the Selling price is £2 (outputs) and the Input price is £1.20 (input) then the value added would be 80p and vat would be 14p. Not 35p.

Whereas the supplier would charge £1.20 less his inputs say 80p and his value added would be 40p – his vat would be 7p so the amount which can legally passed on to the consumer is 21p*. The consumer has been overcharged by using this fraction 14p.

The original 80p was for raw material and is not liable to vat.

So we have established that the "Vat fraction" is incorrect and furthermore it is <u>NOT</u> in the VATA 1994. Therefore illegal!

*This comes from the VATA 1994 Chapter 23 Part I: 1 (2) Vat on any supply of goods or services is a **liability of the person making the supply** and becomes <u>due at the time of the supply.</u> *Now this is not the responsibility or the liability of the customer/ the consumer it is the <u>supplier</u> (Taxpayer). But under the provisions of the Act the business recovers the vat charged at **each stage**(Taxpayer)from the customer/**and passes it on** eventually to the consumer.*

(Taxpayer) is added by me.

Continuing point 4—So why is it when your Takings including vat (17.5%) reaches £75,000—the excess over the threshold is £5,000—the tax should be £744-70. But the HM Revenue & Customs declare you owe £11,170.50. That's because they are ignoring the threshold!!

Now because this fraction is incorrect then when HMRC states you owe 7/47ths on £70,002—they say you owe them £10,425.83. But hold on a minute the threshold is £70,000. So this makes it <u>not liable</u> to vat below that figure and the £2 should be **21p** as shown above therefore where <u>**do**</u> they get the legal right to excessively charge you £10,425.62.

Then following on from this you ask how is this possible and why has it gone on being undetected? Well when you look at a profit and loss account "Excel examples" attached later the Sales for the £70,000 business shows Sales of £70,000. But when you look at the profit and loss account of the £70,00**2** you will find that the Sales appear as £59,576.17. Furthermore, it distorts the gross profit percentage as well. There are 2 reasons for this

1. HMRC made a mistake in assuming that it was a Sales Tax. Furthermore, this was based upon **all** businesses in the chain being standard rated—ignoring exempt, lower rate & zero rates.
2. They were working backwards incorrectly, because the **LAW** says passing on what is paid. <u>Not deducting</u> what you have paid.

Now because you are paying a Sales Tax as we have demonstrated above—your suppliers are also charging you a Sales tax. But the other thing which is being hidden from you is the effect of charging you vat on your Exempt inputs—Rates, Rent, Water rates, Bank Interest, Bank charges, Insurance and Postage. Even when you annually licence your business car you are virtually paying £35 tax (vat/sales tax). Furthermore, you are overpaying 12.5% on your Gas & Electricity.

The "Excel" spreadsheet synopsis of a Profit & Loss Account explains this where we illustrate the £70,000 Turnover compared to the £70,002 Turnover. See "Threshold Diagram"

Then we give other examples of different businesses where the rates of tax are different and the affect it has on those businesses.

We also give an example of how much you must make to return your net income to what it was until you registered.

In the meantime it states in the VATA 1994 if you have overpaid vat you can only recover the last 6 years. £55,039. That's if it is a legitimate tax—but with the Threshold the tax paid below it is not legal. <u>Prove this is wrong!</u> So now we refer to the officially recognised tax authority which is "Tolley's" Value added Tax book from which these figures are obtained . . . .

	Turnover limit inc tax	Tax Rate	Over Paid	
1990-91	£25,400	15%	£3,313	
1991-92	£35,000	17.5%	£5213	
1992-93	£36,600	17.5%	£5451	
1993-94	£37,600	17.5%	£5600	
1994-95	£45,000	17.5%	£6702	
1995-96	£46,000	17.5%	£6851	
1996-97	£48,000	17.5%	£7149	
1997-98	£49,000	17.5%	£7298	
1998-99	£50,000	17.5%	£7447	
1999-00	£51,000	17.5%	£7596	
2000-01	£52,000	17.5%	£7745	
2001-02	£54,000	17.5%	£8042	
2002-03	£55,000	17.5%	£8191	
2003-04	£56,000	17.5%	£8340	
2004-05	£58,000	17.5%	£8638	
2005-06	£60,000	17.5%	£8936	
2006-07	£61,000	17.5%	£9085	
2007-08	£64,000	17.5%	£9532	
2008-09	£67,000	17.5%	£9979	
2009-10	£68,000	15%	£8869	
2010-11	£70,000			£55,039
		Total	£149,977	

The Thresholds can also be located on http://customs.hmrc.gov.uk/channelsPortalWebApp/channelsPortalWebApp.portal?_nfpb=true&_pageLabel=pageVAT_ShowContent&id=HMCE_CL_000081&propertyType=document#P24_1044

We know that the business has to register but nowhere does it say you have to pay below the threshold when you do! Furthermore, it would be discrimination against legitimate businesses when we know that so many small businesses stay below to avoid the VAT. For example I was informed about a Bed & Breakfast boarding house which closed for 3 to 4 months of the year, when its income met the threshold. Then it would pass any business it got to another B&B and collected a 10% commission for referring business. Incidentally, the amounts above may seem high but they were collected under false pretences—secondly, if they are refundable then they would be liable to income taxation. Since the profits for those years would have been understated!

However, look on the positive side—paying this back to small business would boost the economy. More money could be spent on business improvements, hiring more staff, etc.—without recourse to Banks for approval.

Alex J. Dyball

As a current point we would add the Conservative have now provided a new £40,000 **Threshold** upper limit on Family Credit—except it has a negative effect.

Newspaper evidence

We have on file clippings from newspapers which we would need permission to reprint. So we are giving précis's instead.

Our first clipping was dated February 1995. It was reported that £2.4Billion was written off by the taxman for arrears, for the year 1993/94 £819million in vat. 115,000 small businesses made bankrupt. There were 1.6 registered businesses for that period. Who were entitled to the threshold allowance? Threshold that year was £37,600 so vat overpayment was £5,600 per business £8,960,000,000.

Also among the clippings we have articles that points out one of our biggest problems in the educational system to-day—we know there are adverts on TV by "National *Westminster Bank" going into schools with the intentions of advertising their part to* educate young students to the depositing their savings and money into a Bank Account. But this subject should be taught in its entirety—Investing money, return on investments, etc. It also illustrates another problem—The "Babylonian System" the present European structure is to enslave everyone. There is a poverty trap encumbering the working man. The Labour Government tried to mitigate the problem by introducing the "**Family Tax Credits**". The person on Welfare cannot survive on the money they earn—Oh! They get Free Rent & Rates, etc. but to exist they have to do something to get money.—They turn to crime, drugs, etc. When they are lucky they get a job—but once they go over the 16 hours and start earning more their FTC is reduced. So they are virtually working extra for nothing. The minimum wage is built into the system too—all that does is increase the price of goods all along the line—and of course the EEC & HMRC collect more in vat revenues. Satan has always regulated you by a system of bondage, based upon ignorance and unbelief or lack of knowledge. Whereas, God's system is to increase prosperity, he empowers people—in his parables if you did well he rewarded you with more responsibility—he emphasised that people must work. He also said the more you sow the more you would reap. Joseph ran the biggest economy in Egypt and he did it by saving for a rainy day not by spending future income. He rewarded people for results. The only people in our society being rewarded are the tax collectors and the bankers.

Galatians 5: 1 "Stand fast therefore in the liberty by which Christ has made us free and do not be entangled again with a yoke of bondage" (Babylonian system)

As a side note, according to articles in the press Gordon Ramsey, Anthony Worrall Thompson, Jamie Oliver, Paul Rankin, to name a few have all had a brush in with HMRC and faced bankruptcies so there must be something basically wrong with the system? Now in their positions and with their resources to hire the best Accountant you would have thought they would be immune but the fact is the "Vat Fraction" is their problem too. (Incidentally enquiries to the Institute of Chartered Accountants professional body will not answer the query concerning VAT fraction and a Sales Tax)

Again this emphasises the plight of the Catering Industry—I have news clipping from 1997 which states takings have risen 25% in 5 years. (*That means prices have risen not that people are eating out more but stress)* "95% of restaurants **CLOSE** or change hands within two years" a comment made by Neville Abraham, vice Chairman of the Restaurants Association of Great Britain However, I disagree with the reported comment that it is bad management and poor quality of staff. This is trying to generalise—restaurants are going out of business because of the Value Added Tax—which as we have said before is a Sales tax and our opinion is confirmed by Encarta. But in fact it is a miscarriage of the law. With the education in schools lacking in cookery—the supermarkets promoting ready meals/ TV dinners, there is still a market for good wholesome food and restaurants. Furthermore, the introduction of the minimum wage has alleviated cheap labour. But along with the minimum wage they should have introduced a level of efficiency, productivity and responsibility. No two workers are the same and attitude to work in this country is abysmal—they have to get paid a set minimum wage whether they are convivial to customers or not. No two workers are entitled to be paid equal—again it is a Government control system.

It is in France too! I have another newspaper article of September 2008 where it proves this problem is not isolated to the UK but also to France. "It states that 3,000 restaurants in France have gone bust due to the Credit Crunch in the first half of 2008" But according to statistics the Credit Crunch started in final quarter of 2008. Accordingly it says 1782 Traditional French Restaurants January to June 2008 closed. In the same period in 2007(1428), Also small cafes bankrupted had a 56% increase but no figures (but it tells me it is the same problem as in the UK.) Furthermore, French fast food restaurants bankruptcies were up 19% too. This was only the bankruptcies in the Euler Hermes Insurance Company report "this was outright bankruptcies and many other restaurateurs or café owners are retiring or selling up.

The French refer to vat @19.6% and in their food shops the rate of vat is 5.5%—But again we get back to the way the system works. The 19.6% is a Sales tax and the 5.5% is a purchase tax and they deduct it as an input tax. Whereas the EEC law says pass on what has been paid. The restaurant is therefore cheating the public out of 14.1% and/or the Restaurant is paying it.

The article also states that "Turnover has fallen by 20%" but wages have been increased each year because of the minimum wage—Rents and Rates have all increased. With Vat at 19.6% the reduction in Turnover reduces right down to the bottom line—So if the business was making a net profit of 10% it would be completely annihilated.

The French Government tried to persuade the EU to deliver on a promise they had made to the catering industry by President Jacques Chirac six years ago of a cut from 19.6% to 5.5% President Sarkozy has revived the idea but it is blocked by Brussels.(see spread sheet attached depicting our estimation of French Profit and Loss Account).

General observation by author. But at this point I would like to make an observation in the UK—International Franchisee are still expanding, whilst their prices are cheaper than anyone else and there are two sharers in their business—the franchisor commitment and the capital return to the Franchisee. I once asked a vat inspector if I could see a copy of a Vat return from any of the big operators e.g. Burger King, Harry Ramsden, etc. But he said there was customer confidentiality—but I would also draw your attention that the fastest Fish & Chip chain in the UK which is expanding "Deep Blue Restaurants Ltd" has 25 shops in the south of England" details from their website. Started in 2006 their financial director Dave King was financial director with an International franchisor. I wonder if that would be related to retained profits by paying VAT the way I have proposed—which abides by the law and my way of working out value added is correct according to Professor John Kay LSE.(I have this confirmed to me by him in writing).

While we are on this subject concerning Bankruptcies—in my own business—when we started there was a fish market in Belfast with over 12 suppliers—now there is only 3 and no market. The reason being these wholesalers have had to absorb losses of the takeaways—the fish quota pushed up prices by making the commodity too scarce.

As I have pointed out in my spread sheet details the Vat does not appear in the records and the Sales figures reported are after "Skimming" 15% off the top. No doubt the HMRC learnt this from the underworld? The vat liability does not appear on **any** balance sheet as a separate creditor.

Alex J. Dyball

DIFFERENCE BETWEEN UNREGISTERED AND REGISTERED SIMPLE EXAMPLE.

Unregistered Business			Registered Business		
Chocolate Bar			Same Chocolate Bar		
Sell	£1.50		Sells same	£1.50	
Tax	0		Tax (7/47ths)	.22p	
Net Income	£1.50		Net Income	£1.28	
Cost .50p			Cost	.50p	
Input tax .09p	.59p		Input tax .09p	.59p	
Gross Profit	.91p	61%	Gross Profit	.69p	54%
HMRC collects	.09p		HMRC collects	.22p	

Now HMRC tell us it is a consumer tax but the registered business is paying the extra 13p – 7% - the customer is still paying £1.50. This is financial discrimination!

The above illustrates another point we covered earlier about distinguishing between a registered and non-registered business

Chapter 5

Personal Investing.

I occasionally invest in stocks and shares, my reasoning being they sometimes give a better return on savings than putting money in a Building Society or Fixed Interest accounts. Mainly, I stick to well-known shares such as Marks & Spencer Ltd. Compass Group, etc. Furthermore, I like to stick to what I know. For example when I started up in Fish & Chips I bought shares in Harry Ramsden and J. Bibby. (Two companies now swallowed up by takeovers) I chose Harry Ramsden to get a copy of their Accounts and was thus able to construct prices in my own shop to ensure I made a reasonable profit—in keeping with the same type of business. Also as a shareholder I was able to look round their operation in Guiseley, near Leeds, Yorkshire.

You will also notice the more lucrative businesses on the Stock exchange are Banks, Pharmaceutical companies both Vat exempt. Supermarkets zero rated and Oil Companies, Utilities companies lower rated for vat. Also as stated earlier other businesses are subsidising their EEC contribution So when I discovered the mistake being made by HMRC concerning VAT—I picked up an article in the newspaper about "Fishworks PLC" went to the internet and the following site:—

FishWorks plc Unaudited Interim Results

File Format: PDF/Adobe Acrobat - Quick View
FishWorks plc. ("FishWorks" or "the Group"), the acclaimed local restaurant . . .
*www.**fishworks**.co.uk/media/2007InterimStatementsFinal.pdf -*

Alex J. Dyball

I then proceeded to buy shares—35,000 to be exact. I based my decision on the accounts provided. I reworked them to conform to a true Value added.

When reworked these showed a profit of £187,780 on a £8.65m Turnover quoted in the press but appears as £7.37m on their website. This was for the year 31/7/06 where they posted a **Loss of £32,000** for income tax purposes after adjusting for depreciation etc. Since value added is based upon Cash Flow.

The full reconstruction I used is shown in exhibit 1. This details the inclusion of vat transactions for the year and as you will notice the Total amount HMRC have collected is 14.89% of the figure. £1,289,742. The amount due from the Company should be £641,971.The irony of this example is it had 12 Outlets with catering schools to teach. This has been all dissolved and split up by the receivership. Parts sold on and more people thrown back onto the unemployment system. The company has since been purchased by a private Indian owned Company. No money has been returned to shareholders like me.

If you observe the success of the Indian and Chinese investment in the defunct British Car Manufacturers seems to be successful. Posing the question of how can they make the businesses pay when as British owned they ran at a loss. e. g. Jaguar and MG.

Fishworks Ltd.   30th July 2006

Figures rounded up	Amount	VAT	Total
Purchases	2863854	501174	3365028
Wages	2878130	503673	3381803
Accountancy	52491	9186	61677
Advertising	50000	8750	58750
Bank Charges	13769	2410	16179
Bank Interest	35369	6190	41559
Electricity 5%	20000	1000	21000
Directors Fees	370963	64919	435882
Gas 5%	20000	1000	21000
HP Interest	61981	10847	72828
Insurance	20000	3500	23500
Legal Fees	10000	1750	11750
Maintenance	10000	1750	11750
Motor Expenses	10000	1750	11750
Motor Fuel	35000	6125	41125
Motor Insurance	10000	1750	11750
Postage	500	87.5	587.5
Printing	5000	875	5875
Rates	220000	38500	258500
Rent	440986	77173	518159
Repairs	30000	5250	35250
Road Tax	6510	1139	7649
Stationery	17609	3082	20691
Profit	187780	32861	220641
SALES INCOME	7369942	1284742	8654684
Elect & Gas Adjust		5000	5000
	7369942	1289742	8659684
	85.11%	14.89%	100.00%

From a/c's supplied	
Admin Expense interest	4287121
paid	28187
	4315308
Sales income.	7369942
Interest Rec	37731
	7407673

Figures obtained from www.Fishworks.co.uk

This is how HMRC Vat Liability is construction on Sales			True Liability	
Zero Rated	0%	501174		0
Exempt	N/A	141597		0
Lower rate 5% adjust	5%	7000	5%	2000
Std. Rate suppliers	17.50%	38518		38518
Std. Rate this business	17.50%	601453		601453
		1289741		641971 above
Exhibit 1.		Over collected		647770

The above colour codes are a synopsis of the vat liability according to 6th Directive. It also means that this business could only pass on to the consumer £641,971. However, since the Companies prices included Vat it is disclosing a over collection by HMRC on the Company of £647,770.

Chapter 6

UK Poverty Trap.

So what is a poverty trap? Poverty trap is a scenario where people experience poverty due to circumstances beyond their control. The trap becomes cyclical and begins to reinforce itself if steps are not taken to break the cycle. *Wikipedia*

In the case of Vat—a shop, a Plumber, Electrician, etc. Any small business has to register when their turnover reaches £70,000. But when they do reach this figure HMRC say they owe 7/47ths (17.5%) of their Turnover (Sales figure). So on obtaining an increase in revenue to £70,001 their liability according to HMRC is £10,425.68. This is because they have exceeded the Threshold by £1-00. But what is a threshold? (**Chapter 4 explanation**) Now remember THRESHOLD is the Government's own wording in the VATA 1994—23$^{rd.}$ Chapter.

I have taken the turnover of the single self-employed person as £1200 per week which leaves him with a Net income of £360 or £18720 per annum. (a fixed personal wage of £200 for working + profit of £160)

Although there are different configurations between businesses which HMRC use as guidelines when comparing profit and losses in business in our example we have started with an allocation as follows

C.of.Gds @ 30%	Fixed Expense	Staff Wages	NHI chart below	Self-Wages	Subtotal	VAT	Profit	Week income
360	480.00			200	1040.00	0	160.00	360.00
450	480.00	90.00	-1.10	200	1218.90	223.4	57.69	257.69
900	480.00	540.00	26.40	200	2146.40	446.8	406.78	606.78
1057.5	480.00	697.50	43.73	200	2478.73	525	521.26	721.26
1140	480.00	780.00	41.80	200	2641.80	565.96	592.23	792.23
1410	480.00	1050.00	60.50	200	3200.50	700	799.48	999.48
1800	480.00	1440.00	81.40	200	4001.40	893.6	1104.96	1304.96
3000	480.00	2640.00	191.40	200	6511.40	1489.4	1999.20	2199.20

▶	Material content	▶	£360	▶	30%
▶	Fixed Expense content	▶	£480	▶	40%
▶	Wages	▶	£200	▶	16.6%
▶	Profit before Inc. Tax	▶	£160	▶	13.4%
▶	Total Turnover	▶	£1200	▶	100%

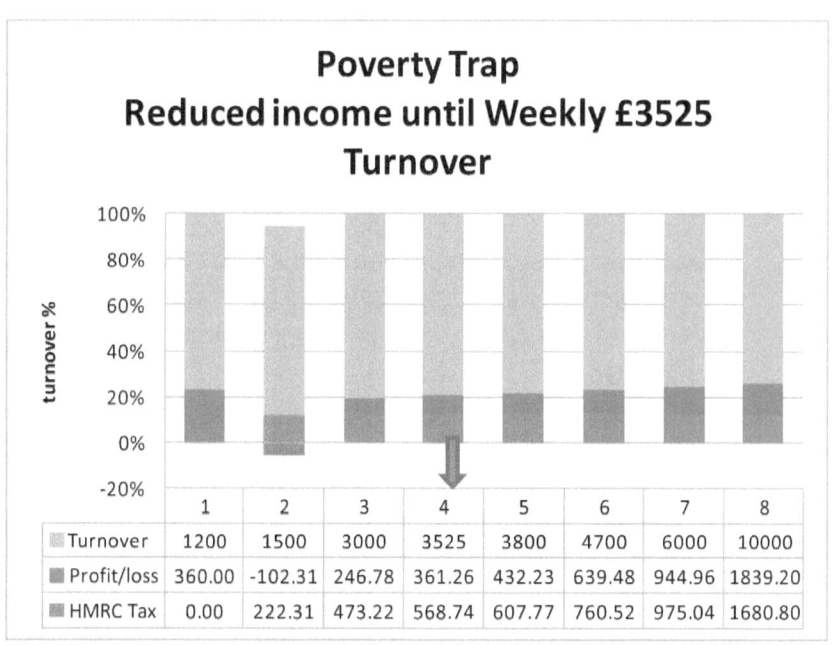

Poverty Trap
Reduced income until Weekly £3525 Turnover

	1	2	3	4	5	6	7	8
Turnover	1200	1500	3000	3525	3800	4700	6000	10000
Profit/loss	360.00	-102.31	246.78	361.26	432.23	639.48	944.96	1839.20
HMRC Tax	0.00	222.31	473.22	568.74	607.77	760.52	975.04	1680.80

HMRC tax is vat + NHI. e. g. Turnover £3525 = vat £525+ NHI £43.73=£568.74. Profit is £361.26 is£721.26 less£360 original profit.

▸ The second column I have increased his business by £300 per week which is £78,000 and above the threshold to pay vat. According to HMRC the business has to pay £11617 vat. However in doing so the self-employed person's income becomes £258 per week and £13416 per annum. (Income tax reduces this to £12028) So at this point it is not worth his while to be self-employed. So then you say to yourself what do I need to earn to get me back to a weekly income of £360—and taking into account you need to pay help to increase your Turnover—It works out at £3,525 per week nearly treble. However, in spite of your earnings being the same your revenue as a percentage of sales has been reduced from 30% (£360/£1200) down to 10% (£361/£3525) Whereas, HMRC income including the extra you have to pay for NHI on the employee's income is 16%. (£569/£3525) So in a nutshell you do all the work, including all the government forms pay yourself £360 and the Government gets £569. Are you mad?

▸ But it gets better Take £10,000 per week and you'll get £1839 (18% on your turnover of £10,000) and the HMRC gets £1681. **But hold on a minute you have to pay income tax on your £1839**—after the **personal allowance threshold of (£6,475) £124.5 per week you pay tax** on £1714.5 per week £719 @ 20% = £143.8+ £995.5 @ 40% = £398.2 = TOTAL Income tax of £542.leaving you with £1297. That means the Government gets £2,223 or 22% (£2,223/£10,000) and your 13% (£1297/£10,000). What an incentive and a poverty trap! **Sure the Government wants you to be self employed**

▸ The Governments excuse is that it is the consumer who pays! But if that were the case why does it say in the VATA 1994 that the business is the **_taxpayer._** Furthermore, it is the business which is **sued** by the HMRC. The biggest instigator of Bankruptcies in the UK.

▸ Spread sheets are useful but another point not taken into account is the fixed expenses. Namely, Rent—Rates—Insurance—Road tax—etc. To take the turnover from £1200 per week to £10,000 per week—would probably need bigger premises, equipment, etc. also it would need customer demand. Another thing which is dampened by Government. Also the law of Diminishing returns also comes into effect. The whiskey industry can testify to that when duty was imposed on it.

▸ Another item which has altered over the years I'm in the Fish & Chip Industry is the quota system—it has made a scarcity and created a built in price increase. Added to which big firms such as "Young's Frozen Foods" are buying the catch before it reaches the ports to supply their factories—They are competing through the supermarkets with a battered frozen item at least a 1/3rd the price of take away shops because they are zero rated. The Government introduces laws in one place (quota) which affects business and taxation in another place.

When a small firm starts up they do not realise the ramifications of Competition—again referring to my own industry—a Local competitor rented a small shop while he was rebuilding his own shop. The new Property and equipment to rebuild cost approximately £400,000. After he was out of the rented property someone else came in and started up in competition to him but undercut all his prices. The two shops are 3 doors apart—but the local council is collecting rates off both shops. I'll say no more> except that is where there should be Government interference!

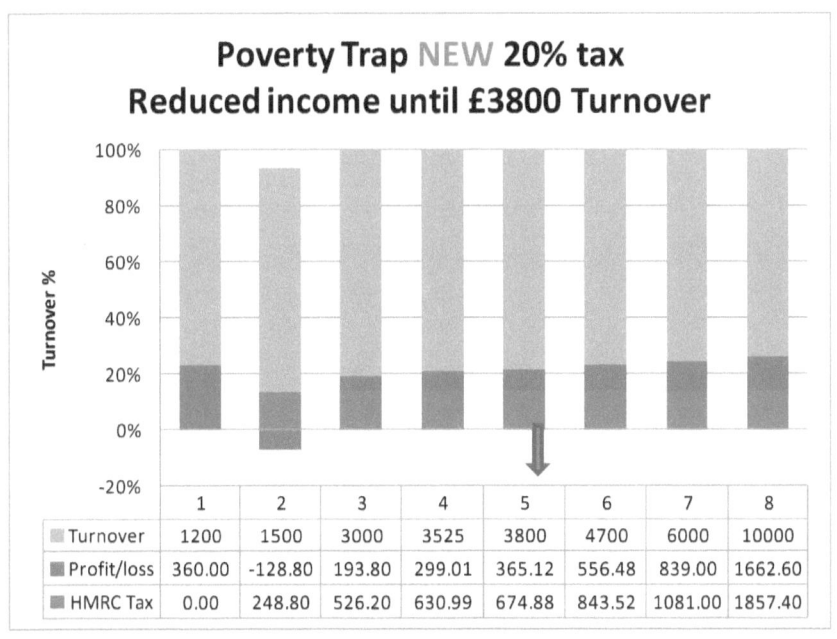

	1	2	3	4	5	6	7	8
Turnover	1200	1500	3000	3525	3800	4700	6000	10000
Profit/loss	360.00	-128.80	193.80	299.01	365.12	556.48	839.00	1662.60
HMRC Tax	0.00	248.80	526.20	630.99	674.88	843.52	1081.00	1857.40

Alex J. Dyball

You can work out your own effects on your income—but notice HMRC gets more than you do from your business every time! No wonder they are encouraging people to go self-employed.

But the HMRC should be aware

Colossians 2 v15. AMP. God disarmed the principalities and power that were ranged against us and made a bold display and public example of them, in triumphing over them in him and in it (the cross)i

Second Section

This section is mathematical and will not be easily understood by persons who are not familiar with figures.

We give examples of Profit and Loss Accounts which round out the details of our observations.

Including a French business example displayed in euros.

If you would like any help constructing the details of your own business—we would be happy to assist you. However we have provided a template for you to complete.

www.vatreduction.co.uk

Comparison of Businesses Taking £70,000 and £70,002

Any Unregisterd Business for VAT
On the P&L account for income tax purposes all that appears is the Grey area. All examples

	INPUTS	Sales tax			OutPUTS	Sales tax	
Cost of Mat	£17,872	£3,128	£21,000	Sales	£70,000	£0	£70,000
Wages	£5,106		£5,106				
Exempt Items	£15,000	£0	£15,000				
Gas & Electric	£2,858	£143	£3,001				
Taxable items	£5,106	£894	£6,000				
	£45,942	£4,164	£50,106				
Profit	£19,894		£19,894				
	£65,836	£4,164	£70,000				

> Although this business is unregistered its Selling prices are the same as a registered business - so it is reclaiming the input vat from the consumer.So recovers the input tax as if it was registered On the P&L account for income tax purposes all that appears is the Grey area.

4164/70,000   Sales Tax perc%   5.95%

The figures below create a small business poverty trap!

	This is the vat position for the registered business taking £2 extra						
		Sales tax					
Cost of Materials	£17,872	£3,128	£21,000			Sales tax	
				Sales	£59,576	£10,426	£70,002
Wages	£5,106	£894	£6,000				
Exempt Items	£15,000	£0	£15,000				
Gas & Electric	£2,858	£143	£3,001				
Taxable items	£5,106	£894	£6,000				
	£45,942	£5,058	£51,000				
Profit	£13,634	£2,386	£16,020				
	£59,576	£7,444	£67,020				

> Notice here the business has taken the same amount of sales plus £2. They have been able to reclaim the vat inputs. But in spite of that their profit has declined from £19,000 to £13634. So this is a loss of £5366 for taking an extra £2. Plus an overpayment of vat on exempt items of £2625 and the lower rate of £367 = £2982.
> Total loss.................. £8,348

HMRC state your liability is	£10,426
Less input tax	£4,164
	£6,262

But your liability should be	£70,002	£10,426
Less Threshold	£70,000	-£10,426
Net Liability	£2	£0.298
Construction of overpayment		
Exempt item	£2,625	
Gas & Electric	£357	
	£2,982	
Suppliers	£4,164	VAT
This business	£3,280	£7,444
	£10,426	

£7,444/£70,002   Sales Tax perc%   10.63%

> The VATA says you have to register for vat at £70,000 current year. The Government called it a Threshold. Unregistered and Registered sell same items so they sell at the same price because of competition. Therefore , the Government is discrimminating between the two. Since the VAT does not appear upon the recorded P&L a/cs They are Skimming. (not appearing in their accounts) This is illegal!

Result when a Sales Tax is made into a Value Added tax

To bring the businesss back to its original prosperity for the owners

Amount to be sold to obtain same profit as unregistered £19,000

On the P&L account for income tax purposes all that appears is the Grey area. All examples			

		Sales tax					
Cost of Materials	£24,900	**£4,358**	29,258			Sales tax	
				Sales	£83,000	£14,525	£97,525
Wages	£7,113	£1,245	8,358				
Exempt Items	£20,898	£0	20,898				
Gas & Electric	£3,976	**£199**	4,174				
Taxable items	£7,113	**£1,245**	8,358				
	£64,000	£7,046	71,046				
Profit	£19,000	£3,325	22,325				
	£83,000	£10,371	93,371				

To obtain the same profit for the owners of the business before they registered for Vat - which was £19,000. They would have to increase their business to £97,525.
(£97,525-£70,000 =£27525/ £70,000) An increase of 39%. However, ignoring the Threshold their VAT Liability which they can legally pass on to the public is £10,371. As a fraction of the sales figure or HMRC "Vat fraction" This would be 10371/93371 or 11.1% Sales tax.
All inputs have been kept in proportion to the original as a percentage of Sales.

HMRC state your liability is	£14,525
Less input tax	**£5,801**
	£8,724

But your liability should be	£97,525	14,525
Less Threshold	£70,000	-10,426
Net Liability	£27,525	4,100
Construction of overpayment		
Exempt item	£3,657	
Gas & Electric	£497	
	£4,154	
Suppliers	**£5,801**	VAT
This business	£4,100	9,901

But since the threshold is £70,000	14,525
The vat from this bus & Suppliers	**9,901**
Refund due	4,624

To verify Income & Expenses to Gross Sales

Expenses and Purchases	£93,371 New Charges to consumer as a VAT in law.
Overcharge of Vat	£4,154
Old Gross Sales	£97,525

However we would point out to increase business by 39% would need more Staff
It may also need more space and increased Rent and Rates

Solicitor or Hairdressers Salon Taking £5076 per week
On the P&L account for income tax purposes all that appears is the Grey area. All examples

Replace your own figures from last years profit & Loss Account to give you your overpayment

		Sales tax				Sales tax	
Cost of Materials	£21,600	£3,780	£25,380				
				Sales	£216,000	£37,800	£253,800
Wages/Salaries	£79,200	£13,860	£93,060				
Exempt Items	£35,000	£0	£35,000				
Gas & Electric	£12,000	£600	£12,600				
Taxable items	£18,000	£3,150	£21,150				
	£165,800	£21,390	£187,190				
Profit	£50,200	£8,785	£58,985				
	£216,000	£30,175	£246,175				

HMRC state your liability is £37,800
Less input tax £7,530
£30,270

Since this is a labour intensive business you pay vat on Wages and profits. Now because HMRC work on 7/47ths of selling price it works out at £37,800. But in effect you only have to pass on your vat + suppliers vat. You have overpaid £7,625 on reduced rate vat and exempt items plus recovering for the Threshold £10,426 . Overpayment is £18,051. Since you can only legally pass on to the consumer the vat you have paid plus your own liability.

But your liability should be	£253,800	£37,801
Less Threshold	£70,000	-£10,426
Net Liability	£183,800	£27,375

Construction of overpayment			Per% of Sales	7.78%
Exempt item	£6,125			£37,800
Gas & Electric	£1,500		Threshold	-£10,426
Overpaid	£7,625		Overpayment	-£7,625
Suppliers	£7,530	VAT		£19,749
This business	£12,219	£19,749		

Cost of Materials	Exempt Items	Taxable items
Combs	Bank Charges	Accountancy
Conditioner	Bank Interest	Advertising
Hair Dyes	Finance HP	Cleaning
Hairdryers	Insurance	Entertainment
Scissors	Postage	Legal Fees
Shampoo	Rates	Motor Expenses
etc	Rent	Renewals
Books	Water Rates	Repairs
Court Costs		Telephone
Legal Documents		
Stationery		

Correct allocation of vat and who pays it.

	Inputs			Outputs		Total	Less	Pays
	Buys	Vat	Total Cost	Sells	Vat	Sell Price	Input	HMRC
Material				£21,600	3780	25380	21600	3780
Manufacturer	£21,600	£3,780	£25,380	£100,800	£17,640	118440	£79,200	13860
Wages/Salaries	100800	17640	118440	£118,800	£20,790	£139,590	£18,000	3150
Gas & Electric	118800	20790	139590	£130,800	£21,390	£152,190	12000	£600
Exempt items	130800	21390	152190	£165,800	£21,390	187190	35000	£0
Profit	165800	21390	187190	£216,000	£30,175	246175	50200	£8,785
Customers	216000	30175	246175					30175
					Threshold	70000	-10426	19749

Result when a Sales Tax is made into a Value Added tax

Convenience Store

Convenience Store taking £10,000 per week Including VAT
On the P&L account for income tax purposes all that appears is the Grey area. All examples

		Sales tax				Sales tax		
Replace your own figures from last years profit & Loss Account to give you your overpayment								
Cost of Materials	£102,000	**£17,850**	£119,850					
Zero rated	£80,000	£0	£80,000 Sales	£255,319	£44,681	£300,000 Taxable	
Wages/Salaries	£100,000	£17,500	£117,500 Zero	£200,000		£200,000	
Exempt Items	£35,000	£0	£35,000		13375	£13,375	
Gas & Electric	£12,000	**£600**	£12,600				
Taxable items	£18,000	**£3,150**	£21,150				
	£347,000	£39,100	£386,100				
Profit	£108,319	£18,956	£127,275				
	£455,319	£58,056	£513,375		£455,319	£58,056	£513,375

HMRC state your liability is	£44,681	
Less input tax	£58,056	
	-£13,375	
But your liability should be	£300,000	£44,682
Less Threshold	£70,000	-£10,426
Net Liability	£230,000	£34,256

This account is slightly different because a Convenience Store has to charge Vat on its profit as it is part of its value added **but** some of this includes the zero rated items. So in this case the Vat Liability is only 7/47ths of the standard rated items.You must include the zero rated when you are calculating to register but it is a rate of tax which is Zero. If the Sales were "Exempt" it would be a different matter. So what is this entry of £13375 VAT/Sales tax on the income side of our P&L a/c? Well it is the total expense Vat £58,056. Less HMRC calculation on taxable sales £44,681.

Construction of overpayment

Zero Rated Purch	£14,000
Exempt item	£6,125
Gas & Electric	£1,500
	£21,625
Suppliers	**£21,600**
This business	**£26,030** £47,630

Per% of Sales   14.89%

Cost of Materials	Exempt Items	Taxable items	Zero rated
Cigarettes	Bank Charges	Accountancy	Bread & Cakes
Cosmetics	Bank Interest	Advertising	Fruit
Minerals	Finance HP	Cleaning Mat	Tin Food
Postcards	Insurance	Entertainment	Vegetables
Shampoo	Postage	Legal Fees	etc
Washing Pwder	Rates	Motor Expenses	
etc	Rent	Renewals	
	Water Rates	Repairs	
		Telephone	

Correct allocation of vat and who pays it.

	Inputs Buys	Vat	Total Cost	Outputs Sells	Vat	Total Sell Price	Less Input	Pays HMRC
Material Zero rated				£80,000	£0	80000	80000	0
Material Taxable	£80,000	£0	80000	£182,000	£17,850	199850	£119,850	17850
Taxable items	182,000	17850	199850	£200,000	£21,000	221000	£18,000	3150
Gas & Electric	200000	21000	221000	£212,000	£21,600	233600	12000	600
Exempt items	212000	21600	233600	£247,000	£21,600	268600	35000	£0
Profit + Wages	247,000	21,600	268,600	455,319	58,056	513,375	208,319	36,456
Customers	455,319	58,056	513,375					58,056
						Threshold	-10,426	47,630

Result when a Sales Tax is made into a Value Added tax

Caterer

Catering or Restaurant taking £10,000 per week Including VAT
On the P&L account for income tax purposes all that appears is the Grey area. All examples

Replace your own figures from last years profit & Loss Account to give you your overpayment

		Sales tax					
Cost of Materials	£5,000	£875	£5,875		Sales tax		
Zero rated	£165,500	£0	£165,500 Sales	£425,532	£74,468	£500,000 Taxable
Wages/Salaries	£100,000	£17,500	£117,500			
Exempt Items	£35,000	£0	£35,000			
Gas & Electric	£12,000	£600	£12,600			
Taxable items	£18,000	£3,150	£21,150			
	£335,500	£22,125	£357,625			
Profit	£90,032	£15,756	£105,788			
	£425,532	£37,881	£463,413	£425,532	£74,468	£500,000

HMRC state your liability is	£74,468	
Less input tax	£37,881	
	£36,588	
But your liability should be	£500,000	£74,470
Less Threshold	£70,000	-£10,426
Net Liability	£430,000	£64,044

Taxable items	Exempt Items	Zero rated
Accountancy	Bank Charges	Baps
Advertising	Bank Interest	Beefburgers
Cleaning Mat	Finance HP	Fish
Entertainment	Insurance	Flour
Legal Fees	Postage	Oil
Motor Expenses	Rates	Onions
Renewals	Rent	Potatoes
Repairs	Water Rates	etc
Telephone		

Construction of overpayment

Zero rated	£28,962.50	
Exempt item	£6,125	
Gas & Electric	£1,500	
	£36,588	
Suppliers	£4,625	VAT
This business	£33,256	£37,881

Prec% Sales   7.58%

Cost of Materials
   Minerals

Correct allocation of vat and who pays it.

	Inputs			Outputs		Total		Less	Pays
	Buys	Vat	Total Cost	Sells	Vat	Sell Price	Input	HMRC
Material Zero rated				£165,500	£0	165500	165500	0
Material Taxable	165500	0	165500	£170,500	£875	171375	£5,000	875
Gas & Electric	£170,500	£875	171375	£182,500	£1,475	183975	12000	600
Exempt items	182500	1475	183975	£217,500	£1,475	218975	35000	0
Taxable items	217,500	1,475	218,975	235,500	4,625	240,125	18,000	3150
Profit + Wages	£235,500	£4,625	240,125	425,532	37,881	463,413	190,032	33255.6
Customers	425,532	37,881	463,413					37,881
						Threshold	-£10,426	£27,455

Result when a Sales Tax is made into a Value Added tax

Caterers Figures re-worked to demonstrate for people who can't calculate across
Also to allow for the theshold

Correct allocation of vat and who pays it.

	Inputs			Outputs		Total	Less	Pays
	Buys	Vat	Total Cost	Sells	Vat	Sell Price	Input	HMRC
Material Zero rated	165500	0	0	165500	0	165500	165500	0
Material Taxable	170500	875	165500	170500	875	171375	5000	875
Gas & Electric	182500	1475	171375	182500	1475	183975	12000	600
Exempt items	217500	1475	183975	217500	1475	218975	35000	0
Taxable items	235500	4625	218975	235500	4625	240125	18000	3150
Profit + Wages	425532	37880.6	240125	425532	37880.6	463412.6	190032	33255.6
Customers	425532	37880.6	463412.6	425532		463412.6		37880.6
70000 Threshold	59575	10425	70000					-10425
								27455.6

	Material Zero	Material Taxable	Gas/electic	Exempt	Taxable	Profit/wages
Sell	165500	171375	183975	218975	240125	463412.6
Input 40%	66200	165500	171375	183975	218975	240125
Value added inc vat	99300	5875	12600	35000	21150	223287.6
Rate of Vat	0	17.50%	5%	0	17.50%	17.50%
Goods		£5,000	£12,000	£12,000	£17,999	£190,031
Tax paid to HMRC		£875	£875	£600	£3,150	£33,255

Vat as a percentage of SELLING PRICE   8.17%

Vat as a percentage of SELLING PRICE less Threshold   5.92%

£37,880

Looking at the Caterer from a micro perspective

Mineral		Fish	
Mineral Sells @	£2.35	Fish Sells @	£2.35
Cost inc vat zero	£1.175	Cost inc vat	£1.175
Value added inc vat	£1.175	V added inc vat	£1.35
V.A. 40/47ths	£1.00	V.A. 40/47ths	£1.15
14.89%	£0.175	14.89%	£0.20
Paid by supplier	£0.175	Paid by supplier	£0.00
Total rec'd HMRC	£0.35		£0.20

However, HMRC say we owe them 35p on Fish.
If the fishmerchant had charged 17.5p then the
Caterer could pass it on but he didn't. So the difference
arises because 15p extra is being collected from caterer
Now his VA is slightly higher by 15p which equates to 2.234p
extra tax.(7/47ths of 15p = 2.24p) =.175p+0.0224 =.1974p

Calor Gas business selling cylinders of Gas(500x£10 per week)
On the P&L account for income tax purposes all that appears is the Grey area. All examples

		Replace your own figures from last years Profit & Loss Account to give you your overpayment						
		Sales tax					5%	
Cost of Materials	£150,000	**£26,250**	£176,250				Sales tax	
25000 @ £6		£0	£0	Sales	£250,000	£12,500	£262,500	Taxable
Wages/Salaries	£20,000	£1,000	£21,000					
Exempt Items	£15,000	£0	£15,000					
Gas & Electric	£4,000	£200	£4,200			£28,125	£28,125	
Taxable items	£12,000	**£2,100**	£14,100					
	£201,000	£29,550	£230,550					
Profit	£49,000	£2,450	£51,450					
	£250,000	£32,000	£282,000		£250,000	£40,625	£290,625	
		£28,550						
HMRC state your liability is		£12,500			Perc% Sales		12.19%	
Less input tax		£32,000						
		-£19,500						

But your liability should be	£262,500	£39,096.750
Less Threshold	£70,000	-£10,425.800
Net Liability	£192,500	£28,670.950

Construction of overpayment
Zero rated	£0.00
Exempt item	£2,625
Gas & Electric	£500
	£3,125

Suppliers	**£28,550**	VAT
This business	£3,450	£32,000

> Although we ve shown this for Calor Gas. The same would apply to Heating Oil. These are the only businesses which do not pay on their Value added because they reclaim what they pay out from the money they receive. So therefore the overpayment structure does not apply and although the figures show a repayment of £28,125. In fact they do not pay any value added themselves and reclaim £28,550 less £12,500. = £16,050.
> The irony is it is the supplier not the consumer who benefits from the reduced rate of va/sales tax. What this actually does is alter who gets the money - the Distributor

Cost of Materials	Exempt Items	Taxable items
Gas Cylinders	Bank Charges	Accountancy
Heating Oil	Bank Interest	Advertising
	Finance HP	Cleaning Mat
	Insurance	Entertainment
	Postage	Legal Fees
	Rates	Motor Expenses
	Rent	Renewals
	Water Rates	Repairs
		Telephone

Correct allocation of vat and who pays it.

	Inputs			Outputs		Total	Less	Pays
	Buys	Vat	Total Cost	Sells	Vat	Sell Price	Input	HMRC
Material Taxable				£150,000	£26,250	£176,250	£0	£26,250
Gas & Electric	£150,000	£26,250	£176,250	£154,000	£26,450	£180,450	£4,000	£200
Exempt items	£154,000	£26,450	£180,450	£169,000	£26,450	£195,450	£15,000	£0
Taxable items	£169,000	£26,450	£195,450	£181,000	£28,550	£209,550	£12,000	£2,100
Profit + Wages	£181,000	£28,550	£209,550	£250,000	£12,500	£262,500	£69,000	-£16,050
Customers	£250,000	£12,500	£262,500					£12,500
						Threshold	£0	£12,500

Result when a Sales Tax is made into a Value Added tax

Calor Gas business selling cylinders of Gas(500x£10 per week)
On the P&L account for income tax purposes all that appears is the Grey area. All examples
Replace your own figures from last years Profit & Loss Account to give you your overpayment

	Sales tax				5%		
Cost of Materials	£150,000	£7,500	£157,500		Sales tax		
25000 @ £6		£0	£0 Sales	£250,000	£12,500	£262,500	Taxable
Wages/Salaries	£20,000	£1,000	£21,000				
Exempt Items	£15,000	£0	£15,000				
Gas & Electric	£4,000	£200	£4,200				
Taxable items	£12,000	£600	£12,600				
	£201,000	£9,300	£210,300				
Profit	£49,000	£2,450	£51,450				
	£250,000	£11,750	£261,750	£250,000	£12,500	£262,500	
		£8,300					
HMRC state your liability is		£12,500		Perc% Sales		4.48%	
Less input tax		£11,750					
		£750					

But your liability should be	£262,500	£39,096.750
Less Threshold	£70,000	£10,425.800
Net Liability	£192,500	£28,670.950

Construction of overpayment
Zero rated	£0.00
Exempt item	£750
Gas & Electric	£0
	£750

Suppliers	£8,300	VAT
This business	£3,450	£11,750

In this example all Heating Oil and Gas are charged @ 5% and the difference is £750 on the exempt items which - should be excluded at any rate. 6th Directive Article 22 v 4 "the total amount of the exempted **supplies**" Notice difference in allocation affect on Profits

Cost of Materials	Exempt Items	Taxable items
Gas Cylinders	Bank Charges	Accountancy
Heating Oil	Bank Interest	Advertising
	Finance HP	Cleaning Mat
	Insurance	Entertainment
	Postage	Legal Fees
	Rates	Motor Expenses
	Rent	Renewals
	Water Rates	Repairs
		Telephone

To verify the allocation below refer to Chapter 2 EEC Website allocation - this applies to all examples

Correct allocation of vat and who pays it.

	Inputs Buys	Vat	Total Cost	Outputs Sells	Vat	Total Sell Price	Less Input	Pays HMRC
Material Taxable				£150,000	£7,500	£157,500	£0	£7,500
Gas & Electric	£150,000	£7,500	£157,500	£154,000	£7,700	£161,700	£4,000	£200
Exempt items	£154,000	£7,700	£161,700	£169,000	£7,700	£176,700	£15,000	£0
Taxable items	£169,000	£7,700	£176,700	£181,000	£8,300	£189,300	£12,000	£600
Profit + Wages	£181,000	£8,300	£189,300	£250,000	£12,500	£262,500	£69,000	£4,200
Customers	£250,000	£12,500	£262,500					£12,500
						Threshold	-£3,500	£9,000

Result when a Sales Tax is made into a Value Added tax

Secondhand Car/ Antique dealer

Car dealer selling on average 2 Cars per week at £7,500
On the P&L account for income tax purposes all that appears is the Grey area. All examples

Replace your own figures from last years profit & Loss Account to give you your overpayment				
		Sales tax		
Cost of Materials	£50,000	£8,750	£58,750	Sales tax
Zero rated	£400,000	£0	£400,000 Sales	£638,298 £111,702 £750,000 Taxable
Wages/Salaries	£40,000	£7,000	£47,000	
Exempt Items	£35,000	£0	£35,000	
Gas & Electric	£8,000	£400	£8,400	
Taxable items	£18,000	£3,150	£21,150	
	£551,000	£19,300	£570,300	
Profit	£87,298	£15,277	£102,575	
	£638,298	£34,577	£672,875	£638,298 £111,702 £750,000

HMRC state your liability is £111,702
Less input tax £34,577
£77,125

But your liability should be £750,000 £111,705.022
Less Threshold £70,000 -£10,425.800

Net Liability £680,000 £101,279.222
Construction of overpayment
Zero rated £70,000.00
Exempt item £6,125
Gas & Electric £1,000
£77,125

Suppliers £12,300 VAT
This business £22,277 £34,577
£84,250

> This is another business badly affected by HMRC. Since their costs old cars are with private individuals - the vat has already been paid when the car was new. So in affect they are zero rated because of double taxation rules. To byepass this anomalie HMRC charge vat as 7/47ths of Gross Margin. Which above would be £750,000 less £400,000 = £350,000 or £52,128. Whereas as our calculator says it should be £34,577.
> Overpayment £17,551

Perc% Sales   4.61%

Cost of Materials	Exempt Items	Taxable items
Spare Parts	Bank Charges	Accountancy
Tyres	Bank Interest	Advertising
Zero rated	Finance HP	Cleaning Mat
Items	Insurance	Entertainment
Purchased	Postage	Legal Fees
from public	Rates	Motor Expenses
not registerd	Rent	Renewals
for vat	Water Rates	Repairs
		Telephone

Correct allocation of vat and who pays it.

	Inputs Buys	Vat	Total Cost	Outputs Sells	Vat	Total Sell Price	Less Input	Pays HMRC
Material Zero rated				£400,000	£0	400000	400000	0
Material Taxable	£400,000	£0	400000	£450,000	£8,750	458750	£58,750	8750
Gas & Electric	£450,000	£8,750	458750	£458,000	£9,150	467150	8000	400
Exempt items	458000	9150	467150	£493,000	£9,150	502150	35000	0
Taxable items	493,000	9,150	502,150	511,000	12,300	523,300	18,000	3150
Profit + Wages	511,000	12,300	523,300	638,298	34,577	672,875	127,298	22,277
Customers	638,298	34,577	672,875					34,577

Result when a Sales Tax is made into a Value Added tax

52

Comparing Businesses HMRC method
As per VAT 100 FORM

Box number on form	Outputs	Inputs	Value Added	Output Tax	Input tax	Net	Value Added Perc%
	6	7		1	4	5	
Hairdresser/Solicitor	£216,000	£86,600	£129,400	£37,800	£7,530	£30,270	23.39%
Convenience Store	£455,319	£247,000	£208,319	£44,681	£21,600	£23,081	11.08%
Cataer / Restaurant	£425,532	£235,500	£190,032	£74,468	£4,625	£69,843	36.75%
Calor Gas / Heating	£250,000	£181,000	£69,000	£12,500	£28,550	-£16,050	-23.26%

The correct allocation should be (excluding exempt items)

Box number on form	Outputs	Inputs	Value Added	Output Tax	Input tax	Net	This business Perc%	Output Vat
	6	7	A	1	4	5	=B/A	=C/A
						B		
Hairdresser/Solicitor	£216,000	£51,600	£164,400	£19,749	£7,530	£12,219	7.43%	12.01%
Convenience Store	£455,319	£212,000	£243,319	£47,630	£21,600	£26,030	10.70%	19.58%
Caterer / Restaurant	£425,532	£200,500	£225,032	£37,881	£4,625	£33,256	14.78%	16.83%
Calor Gas / Heating	£250,000	£166,000	£84,000	£12,500	£28,550	-£16,050	-19.11%	14.88%

Problem 1 HMRC have not taken **exempt** items off their inputs because they are not part of the Value added.

Problem 2 HMRC have not allowed for the 5% rate on Lighting & Heating . They have actually charged 17.5%

Problem 3 HMRC cannot amalgamate the different vat rates- collectively they are called vat

But compare it to Drinks Spirits, Beers, Minerals & cocktails are all drinks but the Glass is not the same.
Or Fruit - Apples, Pears, Bannanas, Oranges, etc. all have to be treated different.

The Eire Government have a fine example of the way Vat is calculated.
A similar example is produced below.

This is a Sales Tax

	Inputs Buys	Vat	Total Cost	Outputs Sells	Vat	Total Sell Price	Output Less Input	Pays HMRC
					17.50%		Value added	
Manufacturer				100	17.5	117.5	100	17.5
Wholesaler	100	17.5	117.5	200	35	235	100	17.5
Retailer	200	35	235	300	52.5	352.5	100	17.5
Consumer	300	52.5	352.5					52.5
					Perc% Sales		14.89%	

Now the only problem with the above explanation which everyone misses is that to manufacture something you have to have a raw material. Lets say wood. The Trees are free to cut down but they must be dressed for use - So we added another line below for timber merchant.

This is a Value added tax

	Inputs Buys	Vat	Total Cost	Outputs Sells	Vat	Total Sell Price	Output Less Input	Pays HMRC
					17.50%		Output	
Timber Mt	20	0	20	50	5.25	55.25	30	5.25
Manufacturer	50	5.25	55.25	100	14	114	50	8.75
Wholesaler	100	14	114	200	31.5	231.5	100	17.5
Retailer	200	31.5	231.5	300	49	349	100	17.5
Consumer	300	49	349					49
					Perc% Sales		14.04%	
					Difference wood		20	3.5

So what does this prove - because you ignored the base marterial - in this case £20 - it overcharged £3-35.But the cumulative affect is an overcharge of £52-50 less £49 =£3-50

17.50% V - added		Vat
Timber Mt	30	5.25
Manufacturer	50	8.75
Wholesaler	100	17.5
Retailer	100	17.5
Consumer	280	49

This is when all the participitants in the chain are all standard rated. However, in real life scenario all businesses have an exempt , reduced rate or zero rate portion in their construction.
\this template has been reproduced on several businesses to explain where HMRC have been

French Caterer

Catering or Restaurant taking €10,000 per week Including VAT

On the P&L account for income tax purposes all that appears is the Grey area.   All examples

		Replace your own figures from last years profit & Loss Account to give you your overpayment					
		Sales tax				Sales tax	
Cost of Materials	€ 5,000	€ 980	€ 5,980		425,532.00	€ 83,404.27	508,936.27 Taxable
Lower rated	€ 165,500	€ 9,103	€ 174,603 Sales				
Wages/Salaries	€ 100,000	€ 19,600	€ 119,600				
Exempt Items	€ 35,000	€ 0	€ 35,000				
Gas & Electric	€ 12,000	€ 252	€ 12,252				
Taxable items	€ 18,000	€ 3,528	€ 21,528				
	€ 335,500	€ 33,463	€ 368,963				
Profit	€ 90,032	€ 17,646	€ 107,678				
	€ 425,532	€ 51,109	€ 476,641		425,532.00	€ 83,404.27	508,936.27

HMRC state your liability is		€ 83,404.27			
Less input tax		€ 51,108.77		Taxable items	5.5% Rate
		€ 32,295.50		Accountancy	Baps
				Advertising	Beefburgers
But your liability should be		€ 508,936.27	€ 83,399.39	Cleaning Mat	Fish
				Entertainment	Flour
				Legal Fees	Oil
Net Liability		€ 508,936.27	€ 83,399.39	Motor Expenses	Onions
				Renewals	Potatoes
				Repairs	etc
				Telephone	

	Construction of overpayment				
Lower rated	14.10%	€ 23,335.50			
Exempt item	19.60%	€ 6,860.00			
Gas & Electric	17.50%	€ 2,100.00		Exempt Items	
		€ 32,295.50		Bank Charges	
Suppliers		€ 13,862.50	VAT	Bank Interest Prec% Sales	10.04%
This business		€ 37,246.27	€ 51,108.77	Finance HP	
		€ 83,404.27		Insurance	
				Postage	
				Rates	
Cost of Materials				Rent	
Minerals				Water Rates	

Correct allocation of vat and who pays it.

	Inputs			Outputs		Total		Less	Pays
	Buys	Vat	Total Cost	Sells	Vat	Sell Price		Input	HMRC
Material Zero rated				€ 165,500.00	€ 9,103	€ 174,602.50	€ 165,500.00		€ 9,102.50
Material Taxable	€ 165,500.00	€ 9,102.50	€ 174,602.50	€ 170,500.00	€ 980.00	€ 171,480.00	€ 5,000.00		-€ 8,122.50
Gas & Electric	€ 170,500.00	€ 980.00	€ 171,480.00	€ 182,500.00	€ 10,334.50	€ 192,834.50	€ 12,000.00		€ 9,354.50
Exempt items	€ 182,500.00	€ 10,334.50	€ 192,834.50	€ 217,500.00	€ 10,334.50	€ 227,834.50	€ 35,000.00		€ 0.00
Taxable items	€ 217,500.00	€ 10,334.50	€ 227,834.50	€ 235,500.00	€ 4,760.00	€ 240,260.00	€ 18,000.00		-€ 5,574.50
Profit + Wages	€ 235,500.00	€ 4,760.00	€ 240,260.00	€ 425,532.00	€ 51,108.77	€ 476,640.77	€ 190,032.00		€ 46,348.77
Customers	€ 425,532.00	€ 51,108.77	€ 476,640.77						€ 51,108.77

In this example France does not have a threshold - There are 3 rates 19.6%,food 5.5% & we assume Gas& Electricity is 2.1%

Overpayment is	€ 32,295.50

Result when a Sales Tax is made into a Value Added tax

Costings in diagram form **17.50%**

Sales	£70,000
Materials	£17,872
Gas & Elect	£2,858
Exempt items	£15,000
Taxable Exp	£5,106
Wages	£5,106
Profit	**£19,894**
Purchase tax	£4,164
	£70,000

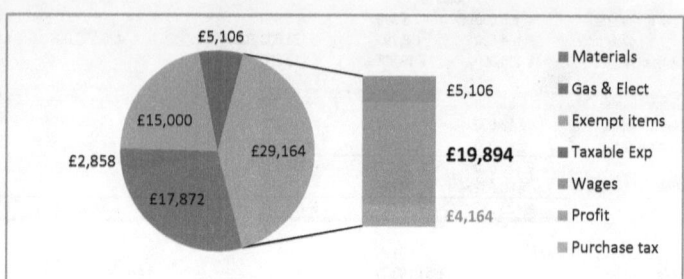

AFTER

Sales	£70,002
Materials	£17,872
Gas & Elect	£2,858
Exempt items	£15,000
Taxable Exp	£5,106
Wages	£5,106
Profit	**£13,634**
Sales tax	£10,426
	£70,002

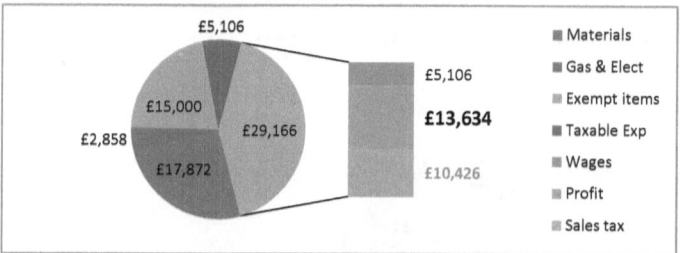

Effect of the Threshold.

These diagrams emphasis the switch in profit for taking **£2** extra. The government looks mainly at the Profit & Loss represented by these figures. The highlighted section on the right has shown an increase in the HMRC Sales tax to £10426 from £4,164. It also explains that the business has had its profits reduced from £19894 to £13634 a drop of £6,260.

Costing a basis for pricing items.

Now the dilemma arises when you are pricing an item to compete with your business competitors. The problem is you increase your price to cover the loss of profit. £6260 + £70002 = £76262 but then you have to increase your Sales tax by £1095 then your price is now £77357. So in effect a £2 increase has become a £7355 price problem or to rephrase it a £6260 loss by the business plus an extra 17.5% on that of £1095 = £7355.

Chancellor's cannot and will not answer this Problem!

Costings in diagram form 20% VAT

BEFORE

Sales	£70,000
Materials	£17,872
Gas & Elect	£2,858
Exempt items	£15,000
Taxable Exp	£5,106
Wages	£5,106
Profit	**£19,320**
Purchase tax	£4,738
	£70,000

AFTER

Sales	£70,002
Materials	£17,872
Gas & Elect	£2,858
Exempt items	£15,000
Taxable Exp	£5,106
Wages	£5,106
Profit	**£12,393**
Sales tax	£11,667
	£70,002

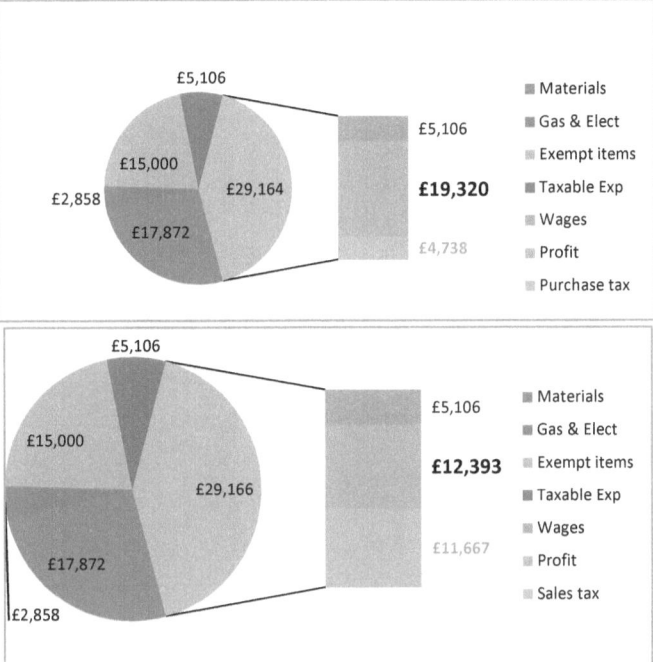

At 17.5% before registering your Profit was £19894
After registering your Profit was £13634
At 20% before registering your Profit was £19320
After registering your Profit was £12393
David Cameron's motto it will pay to work?

FOR WHOM?

How to price an item and calculate your tax liability!

Let us assume you are pricing an item to sell
We'll take something simple like a Washing Machine.
So we start with the parts

20.00%	Cost	Tax	
Motor	60	12	72
Frame	30	6	36
Drum	20	4	24
Switches	20	4	24
Hose	10	2	12
Casing	30	6	36
	170	34	

Vat Rates	
Standard	
Exempt	5%

			Bank Chge	3	3
			Bank Interest	2	2
These are assembled				5	5
Manufacturing	30	6	36 Rent	2	2.4
Spraying	10	2	12 Telphone	2	2.1
Factory OvHd	20	4	24 Light & Heat	2	**0.4** 0.1
Administration	230	**46**	259		47.5
Office Wages	5	1	6 Profit	24	**4.8** 28.8
Insurance	5		5	283	52.3 **335.3**
Rates	5		5		335.3

So during the course of a year you produce 10,000 machines

10000	Cost	Tax	Vat paid	Suppliers	This Business
Material	1700000	340000	340000	340000	
Administration	600000	120000			120000
Office +Phone	70000	14000	14000	14000	
Exempt item	100000	0		1000	1000
Light & Heat	20000	1000		48000	48000
Profit	240000	48000		168000	14000
	2730000	523000	3253000	355000	154000
Less Threshold	70,000	14000		14000	
	2,660,000	509000	3,169,000	355000	509000

HMRC 1/6th calculation (3353000/6) 558833

Overpaid by this business 49833

Customers are still paying the same amount for the machine **£335.30**

Now HMRC state that the business owes them 1/6th of the selling price -£335-30. This amounts to **£55.88.**

Over charge is

Exempt items £20/6 = £ 3.33

Lt & Heat 15%extra 30p/6 .25

Price below £52.30

£55.88

Notice Taxation is over 2 times the profit - what contribution did HMRC make except create paper work!

Total Rev	0	335.3
Materials	165.3	170
Manu	135.3	30
Taxable Adm	133.3	2
Expt Adm	113.3	20
Lt & Ht	111.3	2
Wage	76.3	35
taxation	24	52.3
Profit	0	**24**

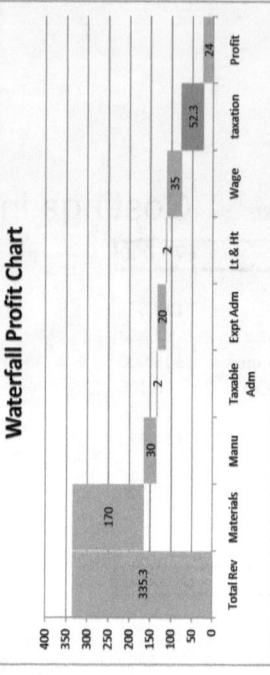

Waterfall Profit Chart

Template for excel Vat calculation

Year 2011   0.2

Any Business					Net	Vat	Total
Expenses	Cost	Vat	Total			=H4*I1	=H4+I4
Rent & Rates			=B4+D4				
Insurance			=B5+D5				
Training Course			=B6+D6				
Bank Charge			=B7+D7				
Clean & Laun		=B8*B44	=B8+D8				
Repairs & Ren		=B9*B44	=B9+D9				
General Exp		=B10*B44	=B10+D10				
Equipt Rent		=B11*B44	=B11+D11				
C.O.Mat		0	=B12+D12				
PPS & Advert		=B13*B44	=B13+D13				
Legal Fees		=B14*B44	=B14+D14				
Petrol		=B15*B44	=B15+D15				
Light + Heat 5%		=B16*B46	=B16+D16				
accountancy		=B17*B44	=B17+D17				
Telephone		=B18*B44	=B18+D18				
Wages		0	=B19+D19				
Profit		0	=B20+D20				
Total	=SUM(B4:B20)	=SUM(D4:D20)	=SUM(E4:E20)		Total =SUM(H4:H20)	=SUM(I4:I20)	=SUM(J4:J20)

In the net box above put the Turnover figure of your Accounts

include **Depreciation** in the Profit box because Value added is based on Cash Flow

Vat 100 Form Correct Way

Output tax	(a)	=+G41		
Input tax	(b)	=+D21		
Due to C&E	(c)	=E34-E35		
Ouputs	(d)	=J44		
Inputs	(e)	=SUM(B4:B18)		
Value added	(d)-(e)	=E38-E39	@ 20%	=E41*0.2
This business	Less paid			=+D21
	Amount due			=G41-G42

Reconciliation Vat

Overpayment Vat				vat rate
Zero Rated	=+B12	=I35*K35		0.2
Exempt	=SUM(B4:B7)	=I36*K36		0.2
Electric	=+B16	=I37*K37		0.15
Total Overpaid		=SUM(J35:J37)		
	Due	=+E34		
		=J38+J39		
	Turnover	=B12/H4		
	Threshold	70000		
	Taxable T/O	=E34/H4		
	GP %	=I4/H4		
0.2	net profit %	=B20/H4		
0	Vat %	=E34/H4		
0.05	sales tax %	=I4/H4		
0	This business			

Value added
exempt
low rate 5%
Zero rated

		This is HMRC METHOD				
Taxable		Per Portion	Sales Tax			
Rates						
Zero	Fish	£ 1.00	£0.175		These amounts were	
Zero	Potatoes	£ 0.50	£0.088		not paid. So they	
5%	Gas	£ 0.03	£0.004		cannot be legally	
5%	Electric	£ 0.03	£0.004		passed on to	
exempt	Overhead	£ 0.75	£0.131		consumer. They are	
Standard	Packaging	£ 0.04	£0.007		all 17.5%	
Standard	Wages	£ 1.15	£0.201			
Standard	Profit	£ 0.15	£0.026		This appears as	
		£ 3.64	£0.637		Sales on P&L a/c	
17.50%	Sales tax	£ 0.64				
		£ 4.28			HMRC collects 64p which is 4 times	
	7/47ths of £4-28 is 64p				more than the business 15p	
		The law states PASS on				
		WHAT is PAID				
Taxable		Per Portion	VAT			
Rates			collectable			
Zero	Fish	£ 1.00	£0.000		Individual pricing of Fish & Chips	
Zero	Potatoes	£ 0.50	£0.000			
5%	Gas	£ 0.03	£0.001			
5%	Electric	£ 0.03	£0.001			
exempt	Overhead	£ 0.75	£0.000		HMRC still get more	
Standard	Packaging	£ 0.04	£0.007		than business profit	
Standard	Wages	£ 1.15	£0.201			
Standard	Profit	£ 0.15	£0.026		Value added this	
		£ 3.64	£0.237		business .227p	
	VAT	£ 0.237			24p/£3.88 as fraction = 6/97ths	
		£ 3.88				

Conclusion

The author of this book Alexander John Dyball was born on 7th January 1934. His childhood was in Leatherhead, Surrey, where his father had a Fish & Chip Shop and his Grandfather started in that business when his father was a lad after the First World War. The author was educated at Ewell Castle School. Surrey and then went on to Pitman's College Wimbledon. After leaving school he was apprenticed to a firm of Chartered Accountants F.E. Hawkes & Co. in Regent Street, London. He migrated to Toronto, Canada and worked for the Accountancy firm Johnson & Co. in downtown Queen & Bay Streets were he continued his accountancy studies. He met his wife Morag Elizabeth Weir at the YMCA Toronto. They got married on 19th September 1959. They returned to Toronto but just prior to their wedding Morag's father had taken a stroke and she was fond of him so they decided to return to Northern Ireland in December 1960. They were Christmas shopping in Ballymena and missed their bus to Antrim Town so they went into a Fish & Chip shop owned by Caulfield—Alex realised that he had made better when he worked in school holidays at his father's shop. They researched the area and found that the Ballymena district had 5 shops and there was a population of 15,000(3000 per shop). They set up and opened their first shop on 24th May 1961. Today in May 2011 there are over 50 places you can buy hot take away food and the population on the register is 70,000(1400 per shop). The reason I emphasis customers per shop is the fact that the Rates on each shop has to be apportioned over fewer people. So if the rates on a shop in 1961 were £1,000 it amounted to .33p per customer. (£5,000/15,000). Today the council's income without allowing for inflation and property revaluation it is 71p per customer (£50,000/70,000). Whereas in real terms it is more like £1-50 per customer in added Government overheads—not taking into account lesser services (Bin collection charged separately) and additional charges for water/sewage rates. We mention this because these overheads are uncontrollable and a burden on all businesses and should be a contributing factor in assessing rates.

This has given you a basic background of the writer in business. However, it does not include that up until 1984 he also opened 3 shops in Belfast selling Fish & Chips and a Catering equipment supply business. A Bakery, a Snack bar and another F&C shop in Broughshane. These were affected by the civil unrest and Value added tax.

Also in the course of 10 Years this <u>one</u> business had a 2 year income tax investigation, then the next 2 years VAT investigation(4 consecutive years), a personal tax investigation, my wife was investigated and then another income tax on the same business. The Inland Revenue was only able to charge us £18 because we had over claimed on our personal petrol allowance—that was it!

The beauty of Accountancy and mathematics is you can always verify things. Example: "Bank Reconciliation"—"Trial Balances" etc. So the examples we have submitted we have also in the main verified according to the Guidelines of the Vat phenomenon—passing on what has been paid. Without cheating the businesses or the consumer, which of course would be Fraud if it was done intentionally or was known and covered up, whether against the public or the individual businesses.

Furthermore, I have written this book to correct unfairness and uphold the truth in law because of the affect on society & employment, bankruptcies which were based upon a false premise has been catastrophic since 1972. I have personal knowledge of the bankruptcy procedure since the C&E tried to make me a statistic. I do not write it with any malice aforethought but out of frustration, in my endeavours I bought this to Prime Minister John Major attention in 1995 and I have also contacted Brussels, letters have been answered but the questions ignored and I have been politely told to stop annoying them. In fact I have on file a newspaper clipping which reported 115,000 bankruptcies for the year 1994/95. I also believe there is a correlation between VAT and bankruptcies and if the Government would publish the true findings we would see that the main instigators for bankruptcy are HMRC.

Not only were the 115,000 businesses affected but staff, creditors and undue hardship have prevailed. Furthermore, this has all been passed on to the consumer in high prices . . . .

Recently I asked a businessman what he would do if he had a refund of £149,000 as outlined in my figures—he said he would buy a new car—invest in new equipment, etc. This would increase new car sales without a scrap age scheme. It would increase employment and if the money was left in businesses they would be able to expand. But all the time money is being syphoned off without accountability then it is going down the drain.

Marks & Spencer is world renowned for its reputation as being a good example of the trends in the UK for customers. When I look back over the years I remember when they advertised their products as being 95% British. However, today you will notice their Clothing is from China, Turkey, India, Israel, and other eastern regions. So let's look at another item on the internet concerning GDP.

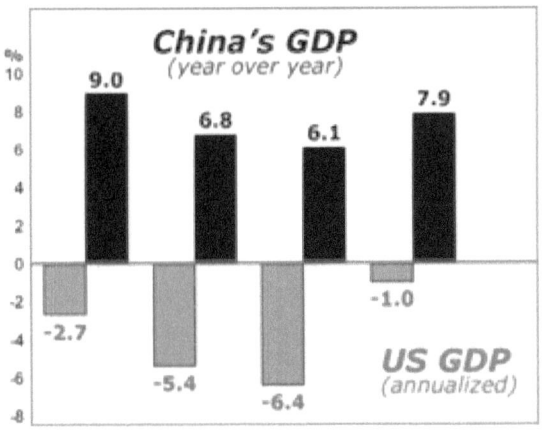

I ask does this signify anything to our politicians.

Does it suggest that we are importing Unemployment?

Does China have to conform to the minimum wage or Holiday pay legislation?

Is China's standard of living of a third world country?

Do they have a balance of payments problem?

Alex J. Dyball

So now you will ask am I advocating our economy should be modelled along Chinese lines. No but what I am saying is EEC regulations are too cumbersome, too complicated and all structured to pay for Government structures and bureaucracy (some of the government offices etc. are too luxurious). Their answer is always more and more taxation, bureaucracy and control. It is the Babylonian system! The politicians complain about the "Black Economy" but this has come about by the rules and regulations they have imposed. The endeavours they have made to cover the needs of the poor, (eliminate poverty has failed) this has been the case since the beginning of time. However, it is like the education system—if people have no incentive to learn and they can get along with hand outs—is it their fault or ours? Is it their responsibility or ours?

However, it must be stressed in the whole of this book that any examples given, my source of information has been the EEC 6th Directive, the VATA 1994 and to implement what I have said does not need any adjustment to the law. If the government can give unauthorised loans to Banks and Building Societies then surely it can give back to business what it has taken illegally.Thank you for your time and we hope this book has enlightened you.

www.vatreduction.co.uk

www.ingramcontent.com/pod-product-compliance
Lightning Source LLC
Chambersburg PA
CBHW021902170526
45157CB00005B/1927